TONY EVANS

STRONGER TOGETHER,

WEAKER APART

HARVEST HOUSE PUBLISHERS
EUGENE, OREGON

Cover design by Bryce Williamson

Cover photo © Trifoneko / Gettyimages

Stronger Together, Weaker Apart
Copyright © 2020 by Tony Evans
Published by Harvest House Publishers
Eugene, Oregon 97408
www.harvesthousepublishers.com

ISBN 978-0-7369-8177-4 (pbk.)
ISBN 978-0-7369-8178-1 (eBook)

Library of Congress Cataloging-in-Publication Data is on file at the Library of Congress, Washington, DC.

Printed in the United States of America

20 21 22 23 24 25 26 27 28 / VP-RD / 10 9 8 7 6 5 4 3 2 1

CONTENTS

ACKNOWLEDGMENTS

I want to thank my friends at Harvest House Publishers for their long-standing partnership in bringing my thoughts, studies, and words to print. I particularly want to thank Bob Hawkins for his friendship over the years, as well as his pursuit of excellence in leading his company. My gratitude belongs to Sherrie Slopianka, Terry Glaspey, Betty Fletcher, and Amber Holcomb. In addition, I want to thank Heather Hair for her skills and insights in collaboration on this manuscript.

THE BATTLE THAT BRINGS US TOGETHER

Division roars louder now than it has in many years past. Everywhere we turn, it seems a new group rises up against another. We are a world divided by a multiplicity of ideas, values, beliefs, preferences, dreams, and expectations. And yet God calls us to live in unity. As the apostle Paul states, "If possible, so far as it depends on you, be at peace with all men" (Romans 12:18).

As kingdom followers of Jesus Christ, we have been chosen to model unity, love, and peace as an alternative to the ways of a world that stands divided. Yet it seems that division often slithers its way into our churches and Christian organizations as well. Satan's overall strategies rarely change—whatever he can divide, he can conquer (Mark 3:24). He accomplishes this division through lies, deception, and destruction (John 10:10). But we must remember that in this battle we are not fighting *for* victory; we are fighting *from* victory. Jesus has already disarmed the rulers and principalities of this rebellion (Colossians 2:15) and has secured the victory for us. We walk in the fullness of this victory by standing in truth, abiding in Christ, resisting the devil and his minions, and waging spiritual warfare according to God's Word.

To say that spiritual warfare happens in this area of oneness with others is an understatement. It's time for us to rise up as the collective body of Christ and call down heaven's authority into the chaos on earth, in order that we might usher in the light, blessings, and favor that defeat the darkness of the enemy.

After all, the call to unity is the great call Christ gave in His high priestly prayer. Shortly before He was arrested and crucified, He prayed,

> I pray also for those who will believe in me through their message, that all of them may be one, Father, just as you are in me and I am in you. May they also be in us so that the world may believe that you have sent me. I have given them the glory that you gave me, that they may be one as we are one—I in them and you in me—so that they may be brought to complete unity. Then the world will know that you sent me and have loved them even as you have loved me (John 17:20-23 NIV).

Just hours before He laid down His life for us, Jesus Christ placed a tremendous emphasis on His desire for His followers to be unified. This isn't something that He is asking us to do only during "Unity Month" or on "Special Oneness Sunday." This is a mandate from our Commander in Chief that we be one with Him and, as a result, one with each other.

Unity is to be our defining marker as kingdom disciples. Jesus said our unity will show the world that God sent Him and that He has loved us as God loves Him. Oneness is not an emotion. Unity is not a song. It is a strategy, responsibility, and approach to advancing God's kingdom agenda and seeing His rule manifested on earth. To live divided (whether at home, work, or church or in our communities, nation, or world) is to bow to Satan rather than the one true God. It is to relinquish our spiritual authority on the altar of discord.

Unity is the keystone of spiritual victory. It must be our goal as followers of Christ if we are to be effective in this call to live as overcomers in spiritual warfare.

The apostle Paul warns us about this ongoing spiritual conflict in several of his epistles, but perhaps most importantly in his letter to the believers in Ephesus, where he also spells out our strategy for winning the battle. That strategy has to do with the armor we wear as we enter into warfare with the enemy of our souls.

> Put on the full armor of God, so that when the day of evil comes, you may be able to stand your ground, and after you have done everything, to stand. Stand firm then, with the belt of truth buckled around your waist, with the breastplate of righteousness in place, and with your feet fitted with the readiness that comes from the gospel of peace. In addition to all this, take up the shield of faith, with which you can extinguish all the flaming arrows of the evil one. Take the helmet of salvation and the sword of the Spirit, which is the word of God.
>
> And pray in the Spirit on all occasions with all kinds of prayers and requests. With this in mind, be alert and always keep on praying for all the Lord's people (Ephesians 6:13-18 NIV).

In my foundational book *Victory in Spiritual Warfare*, I wrote extensively on how we're to engage the enemy with our armor in place. Now I'm offering a collection of powerful prayers that addresses some of the major issues we face in this area of oneness. In addition, there are prayers for favor and requests for God to bless your relationships, workplace, community, church, nation, and our world.

For each topic, you'll find prayers based on each piece of our spiritual armor. Pray the prayers word for word, paraphrase them, or use them as a starting point for crafting your own prayers. The main thing is that you pray.

My goal is that these prayers will act as a starting place for you each day and that when the prayer I've written ends, you will go on praying in your own words about your situation. Remember as you pray that you do not pray as a beggar, but as a warrior for the King of kings. If you need help discovering what I mean by that and how critical it is that you claim your legal rights when you pray, listen to my sermon "Claiming Your Legal Rights" at go.tonyevans.org/prayer.

You have power over your enemy when you pray. You probably have more power than you realize. Your task is to walk in your God-given authority so you are enabled to live out a strong and impactful life in unity with other believers. And you do that through prayer.

The "Everyday" Pieces of Armor

Before we begin, let's take a brief look at each piece of the armor of God. The first three pieces of armor are items we should wear every moment of every day.

The Belt of Truth

Wearing the belt of truth involves realizing that truth is fundamentally God-based knowledge—His viewpoint on a matter—and acknowledging three principles:

1. Truth is comprised of information and facts, but it also includes God's original intent, making it the absolute, objective standard by which reality is measured.

2. Truth has already been predetermined by God.

3. Truth must be accepted internally and then acted on externally.

When you wear the belt of truth and use it by aligning your mind, will, and emotions underneath God's view on a matter—His truth— He will then empower you to overcome the lies of the enemy and fight your spiritual battles with divinely authorized spiritual authority.

The Breastplate of Righteousness

Righteousness has been deposited within us. Our job is to feed it and nourish it with the truth of God so that it expands to surround us with the protection in warfare we desperately need.

When you were first saved, God deposited deep within you a new heart containing all the righteousness that belongs to Jesus Christ. Righteousness is the standard that pleases God. But to benefit from its restoring abilities, you must dig down with the shovel of truth. Then God will release a brand-new you in your decisions and actions, and He will surround you with the secure protection of a breastplate of His righteousness.

Wearing the breastplate of righteousness involves walking securely in your imputed righteousness by virtue of the cross, coming clean with God in your practice of righteousness, and feeding your spirit with the Word of God so that the Spirit will produce the natural out-growth of right living from within you.

The Shoes of Peace

A Roman soldier's shoes were called *caligae*—sandals studded with nails. These nails, known as hobnails, were firmly placed through the sole of the shoe for increased durability and stability. Similar to cleats worn on football and soccer fields today, hobnails gave wearers more traction. It gave them sure footing, increased their mobility in battle, and helped them avoid being knocked down.

So when Paul instructs you to have your feet shod, he is talking about standing firm. When Satan comes, he won't be able to knock you off your feet. You will be able to stand firm because the hobnails on the bottom of your "peace shoes" have dug deep into the solid ground beneath you.

Paul is telling us that we don't have to slide or move with every hit or trial that comes our way. Having our feet shod with the "preparation of the gospel of peace" (Ephesians 6:15) gives us stability so we can resist Satan.

God offers us a peace that reaches beyond what we can comprehend. When we receive and walk in that peace, it settles in as a guard over our hearts and minds (Philippians 4:7). This is the peace that cradles people who have lost their jobs and keeps them from losing their minds. This is the peace that produces praise when there is no paper in the bank. This is the peace that restores hope in the face of failing health. This peace is so powerful that we're instructed to let it control us. We are taught to let it call the shots, make the decisions, and dictate our emotions (Colossians 3:15).

Putting on peace shoes means aligning your soul under the rule of God's Spirit. When you choose to do that, God will release peace into your life because the peace of Christ is now ruling your thoughts and actions. When worry creeps back in, remind yourself that it's lying to you, because God has promised He will provide.

What can you do when peace in your life comes under attack? Take it straight back to the spiritual realm and focus on what God has to say on the matter. When you do that, you will wear shoes unlike any others. You will wear shoes that show the demonic realm, yourself, and others that you are standing firm in God's armor. You will walk without becoming weary, and in those shoes you will find the calming power of peace.

The "Take Up" Pieces of Armor

So far we've looked at three pieces of the armor of God you need to wear in order to be dressed for warfare. You should wear these first three pieces all the time. The "to be" verb in Ephesians 6:14-15—translated *having* in the New American Standard Bible—indicates "at all times." We are always to have the belt of truth, the breastplate of righteousness, and the shoes of the gospel of peace.

The next three pieces are what you are to have at hand, ready to pick up and use when you need them. Paul switches verbs for the next three pieces of the armor, telling us to "take up" the shield of faith, the helmet of salvation, and the sword of the Spirit.

The Shield of Faith

Faith is critical to achieving victory in spiritual warfare. Faith accesses what God has already done or what God plans to do. The shield of faith can also be called the shield that *is* faith because faith itself is the shield.

Scripture is full of verses that describe this weapon of faith and show us where to find it. Hebrews 12:2 tells us that Jesus is the "author and perfecter of faith." In Galatians 2:20, we read that we now live by faith in Christ. "I have been crucified with Christ; and it is no longer I who live, but Christ lives in me; and the life which I now live in the flesh I live by faith in the Son of God, who loved me and gave Himself up for me." First John 5:4 says, "Whatever is born of God overcomes the world; and this is the victory that has overcome the world—our faith."

Faith is a powerful weapon, rooted in Jesus Christ. Jesus embodies all the ingredients of faith, from its creation to its perfection. The key to winning in warfare is this faith.

I define faith in practical terms by saying that faith is acting like God is telling the truth. Another way of saying it is that faith is acting like something is so, even when it is not so, in order that it might be so simply because God said so. Your faith must always be directly tied to an action done in response to a revealed truth—otherwise it is not faith. If you are not willing to do something in response to it, even if that something is as small as simply being still in your soul rather than worrying, then the faith you claim to have is not real. Faith always involves your walk, not just your talk.

Keep in mind, though, that the weapon is not just faith in anything at all. It must be faith in God's truth. Faith is only as valuable as the thing to which it is tied.

For example, if faith is tied to your feelings—how much faith you feel—that faith will be empty. You might feel entirely full of faith but not follow up with actions because you really don't believe in what you say you feel. Faith is always based on your feet—what you do in response to what you believe. Faith is a function of the mind that shows up in your choices and responses to life.

The shield of faith has been given to us to protect us from the deceptive strategies of the enemy. When you use it properly, this shield will enable you to advance against the enemy because you will be confident that what God has said about your situation—through His promises in His Word—is true.

Pick up the shield of faith and grab the victory that has already been won.

The Helmet of Salvation

With the helmet, Paul has once again used a physical example to illustrate a spiritual truth. He demonstrates that just as the brain is the control center for the rest of the body, the mind is the control center for the will and emotions. The mind must be protected with a helmet that's able to absorb being hit by the enemy and even knocked to the ground in the spiritual realm.

One reason we need to wear a helmet is that the enemy is trying to stop us from accomplishing the things God has for us to do. God wants to speak truth into our minds. He sits on high—in the heavenly places—and views the scene below. He can see the field of life much better than we ever could. He can examine the opposition's strategy much better than we can. He has studied the game film much longer than we have. And because of this, God has a few secrets He wants us to hear. They are secrets because often what God has to say to you is meant only for you.

Satan wants to keep us from wearing the helmet of salvation so that his whispers to us become the reality through which we interpret and respond to life.

Everything God is ever going to do for you has already been done. Every healing He will ever give you in your physical body has already been provided. Every opportunity He is ever going to open up for you has already been opened. Every stronghold God is ever going to break in you has already been broken. Every victory you are ever going to experience has already been won. The joy you're desperately seeking already exists. The peace you stay up at night praying and wishing you could enjoy is already present. And the power you need to live the life God has created you to live, you already have. This is because God has already deposited in the heavenly realm "every spiritual blessing" you will ever need (Ephesians 1:3).

Wearing the helmet of salvation means bringing our thoughts in alignment with our new identity in Christ, not our old identity in Adam.

The Sword of the Spirit

This piece of armor stands out from all the others. It's unique because it's the only offensive weapon in the arsenal. Everything else is designed to hold us steady from what the enemy is seeking to bring against us "in the evil day" (Ephesians 6:13). But after God outfits us for battle in order to stand firm, He gives us an additional weapon with which we can attack and advance.

When Paul instructs us to take up the sword of the Spirit, he's letting us know that in this battle, the enemy will sometimes seem to be right in our face—just like a defensive player trying to block a shot in a basketball game. The defender will often stick his body, face, or hands in the offensive player's face so that the offensive player will become disoriented and unable to advance. Satan doesn't want you to send the ball through the net for two points, so to discourage this, he brings his battle—your particular stronghold—as close to you as possible. Oftentimes, that means your battle is being waged within you—in your mind, will, emotions, and body.

Paul says that your offensive weapon is the sword *of the Spirit*. It's not your sword. It's not the church's sword. It's not the sword of good works or even religion. It's not the preacher's sword. This is the sword of the Spirit, and in fact, it's the only weapon we're told that the Spirit uses in the spiritual realm.

When you learn how to use the sword of the Spirit—which is God's Word—you can go on the offensive against the enemy who seeks to destroy you. It doesn't matter whether you're young or old, weak or strong. All you need to know is that the sword in your hand is capable of doing more than you will ever need. You can follow the example of Jesus in the wilderness (Luke 4:1-13) by using the sword of the Spirit to communicate to the enemy specific Scriptures that relate to your specific situation.

The Battle in the Heavenlies

Paul ends his discussion on the armor of God with a clarion call to prayer (Ephesians 6:18). Why? Because prayer is how you get dressed for warfare. Prayer is how you put on the armor. I define prayer as relational communication with God. It is earthly permission for heavenly interference.

Why does prayer often seem difficult to us? Because Satan seeks to direct us away from it. He knows how important it is. He will use every possible means to keep you from seriously communicating with God because he knows what prayer does—it activates heaven's response on your behalf in accordance with the will of God. Prayer never forces God to do what is not His will; rather, it releases from God to us what *is* His will. And it is definitely His will for His people to wage victorious spiritual warfare.

In the book of Daniel we find one of the greatest illustrations of prayer. We see Daniel studying God's Word and then responding to God in prayer based on what he has discovered.

> In the first year of [Darius'] reign, I, Daniel, observed in the books the number of the years which was revealed as the word of the Lord to Jeremiah the prophet for the completion of the desolations of Jerusalem, namely, seventy years. So I gave my attention to the Lord God to seek Him by prayer and supplications, with fasting, sackcloth and ashes (Daniel 9:2-3).

First, Daniel heard the truth of God. Then he talked to God about it. Anytime you talk to God about His Word, you are praying. You don't have to do it on your knees. You can do it while you are working, hanging out with others, washing dishes…whatever. Prayer in your war room is critical, but try not to neglect the need for ongoing prayer throughout the day as well.

Notice what we read later in the chapter.

> Now while I was speaking and praying, and confessing my sin and the sin of my people Israel, and presenting my supplication before the LORD my God in behalf of the holy mountain of my God, while I was still speaking in prayer, then the man Gabriel, whom I had seen in the vision previously, came to me in my extreme weariness about the time of the evening offering. He gave me instruction and talked with me and said, "O Daniel, I have now come forth to give you insight with understanding" (Daniel 9:20-22).

While Daniel prayed, God responded. He sent an angel to help him understand his situation even more. Notice that God did not send the angel to give Daniel understanding *until* Daniel prayed in response to what God had already said. We read, "At the beginning of your supplications the command was issued, and I have come to tell you, for you are highly esteemed; so give heed to the message and gain understanding of the vision" (verse 23). When Daniel began to pray, God gave Gabriel the directive to go to Daniel and give him more understanding. The following chapter gives us greater insight into this occasion.

> Behold, a hand touched me and set me trembling on my hands and knees. He said to me, "O Daniel, man of high esteem, understand the words that I am about to tell you and stand upright, for I have now been sent to you." And when he had spoken this word to me, I stood up trembling. Then he said to me, "Do not be afraid, Daniel, for from the first day that you set your heart on understanding this and on humbling yourself before your God, your words were heard, and I have come in response to your words. But the prince of the kingdom of Persia

was withstanding me for twenty-one days; then behold, Michael, one of the chief princes, came to help me, for I had been left there with the kings of Persia. Now I have come to give you an understanding of what will happen to your people in the latter days, for the vision pertains to the days yet future."

When he had spoken to me according to these words, I turned my face toward the ground and became speechless (Daniel 10:10-15).

When Daniel prayed to God in response to God's words revealed through Jeremiah, God sent a messenger to help Daniel. Twice we read in these two chapters that God sent the angel on the day that Daniel prayed to God about God's already revealed Word. When you are praying according to God's own Word, He hears you and responds. For Daniel, the delay in receiving that response was a result of spiritual warfare in the heavenly realm. Gabriel had been dispatched to go to Daniel with a message from God, but the prince of Persia—a demon—blocked Gabriel from reaching his destination for three weeks.

Your battle is fought in the spiritual realm. You must not fail to realize that. If you do, you will not fight in a way that will bring you victory. We've seen that God heard Daniel's prayer when he first offered it, and God responded immediately. Yet because of the battle taking place in the invisible, spiritual realm, God's response was delayed from reaching its intended destination. In fact, another angel—Michael—was needed to help remove the demon from acting as an obstacle for Gabriel. Ultimately, the prince of Persia got double-teamed so God's message could be delivered to Daniel.

Rarely is a battle overturned and won in a minute. That is why I want to encourage you to continue in prayer. God may not seem to respond immediately, but that's only because of the battles taking place in the heavenlies.

Each piece of armor has a specific use in our warfare against Satan. When put together, they present a mighty defense *and* offense against his tactics. As you use the prayers on the following pages, my hope is that you'll develop the fighting spirit you need to win the battle for unity and that you will join the mighty army of overcomers God is raising up. Your part in carrying out spiritual warfare can change the course of your personal history, your family, your church, your community, and even our nation.

PRAYERS
FOR UNITY

1

UNITY

*I in them and You in Me, that they may be perfected
in unity, so that the world may know that You sent
Me, and loved them, even as You have loved Me.*

JOHN 17:23

The great tragedy today is not so much that our society is still divided along racial, cultural, and class lines, but that God's people, the church, are even more deeply divided. This disunity is Satan's most powerful tool for crippling the influence of Christianity. That is why Jesus prayed that believers might be one in order to overcome the world (John 17:21). When we are one, we will overcome. When we are not one, we will be overrun.

Our tendency to divide ourselves along racial lines is one of the problems we face in achieving unity. Our love for each other demands that we break down these barriers, just as Jesus broke down the traditional divide that existed in His time on earth when He stopped to talk with the woman at the well (John 4:1-26). When we come together in unity, unbelievers will see that Christianity is not a secret and that God alone can jettison centuries of misguided beliefs and traditions. Only then will our unity affect our nation's landscape not only on a personal level, but also in families, churches, and communities at large.

As was the case in Samaria after Jesus witnessed to the woman at the well and she in turn witnessed of Him to her entire community, oneness across racial lines is the greatest evangelistic teaser to the presentation of the gospel that we could ever broadcast both locally and abroad. We read, "From that city many of the Samaritans believed in Him because of the word of the woman who testified, 'He told me all the things that I have done.' So when the Samaritans came to Jesus, they were asking Him to stay with them; and He stayed there two days. Many more believed because of His word" (John 4:39-41).

One of the greatest evangelistic outreaches occurred simply because Jesus took the time to engage and connect with another person from a different background than His own. He even ended up spending a couple days—an entire weekend of time—with the Samaritans. Keep in mind that He had just met them. People from their two cultures didn't even talk to each other. They didn't share water or drink from the same cup. But when Jesus met them, He ended up hanging out in their neighborhood all weekend long.

How do we go from a position of "We don't talk" to "Let's hang out together" so quickly? Easy. When Jesus Christ enters our situations and demonstrates the kingdom principle of oneness through kingdom people, He can turn attitudes that are upside down and make them right side up overnight. He doesn't need a generation to do it. It only takes a minute if He's got people who are willing to live their lives by His rules.

What Jesus did in Samaria is turn distance and doubt—the great divide—into a harmonious fellowship filled with power. When He does that in our lives, we will see Him do things we never dreamed possible. Lifting our blinders, He will enable us to look across the divisions of this life and visualize the unity of His creation, His heart manifested through each unique design. We will see where and how He is working to bring glory to Himself and hope to mankind. Better yet, we will get to experience Him as He pours down His blessings and blows our minds.

Achieving true racial harmony doesn't mean ignoring the very differences that make us interesting. I'm not suggesting we all need to follow one pattern in order to be unified. Our cultural uniqueness is not a bad thing. Jesus didn't dispose of His Jewish passport, trim His beard, and adopt Samaritan slang. Unity does not mean uniformity. Unity means embracing diversity and leveraging a variety of strengths. Through His ministry, Jesus gave us a model of the intentional way we are to regard unity, as well as the depth of engagement we are to have in cross-cultural relationships. Jesus showed value and esteem to an entire group of people through respect and relationship. As His kingdom disciples, we are to do the same.

Put On the Belt of Truth

Lord, thank You for coming to earth and modeling this mandate of unity for us. You have given us the truth of Your Word and revealed how we are to live our lives. Unity is not something beyond our grasp. What Satan divides, he can conquer. Help me model a life of unity like Jesus did. Help me look beyond my own comfort zone and experience the strengths of diversity in Your wonderful creation. Make my voice one that encourages living in the power of unity. In Christ's name and by His authority, I pray this.

Put On the Breastplate of Righteousness

Father, righteousness comes when we live in Your grace, according to Your righteous standard. This standard starts with love and is made visible through hearts that embrace unity. Make my heart righteous through an intentional pursuit of unity. Use my life as a testimony of unity to others. I ask that You give me wisdom on how I can contribute to strengthening the community around me, including this nation. I pray for all of us who call on Your name. May our hearts awaken to the need and calling to live as one under You. In Christ's name and by His authority, I pray this.

Put On the Shoes of Peace

Heavenly Father, when we as Your followers are unified, peace is the natural outcome. When we are divided, conflict and chaos emerge. Of course Satan wants to keep us divided. That's why prayer is so critical, because the pursuit of unity is a spiritual pursuit. We need Your power and divine guidance, as well as Your protection from the enemy, in order to preserve the unity and peace to which You have called us. Help me be an instrument of Your peace in all I do and say—and through the prayers I pray. In Christ's name and by His authority, I pray this.

Take Up the Shield of Faith

Lord, you have told us in 1 Thessalonians 5:16 that we are to "rejoice always." Paul gave us insight into how to make our joy complete, and that is through unity. He said in Philippians 2:2, "Make my joy complete by being of the same mind, maintaining the same love, united in spirit, intent on one purpose." I can live joyfully and in peace when I, in faith, seek unity with others, "intent on one purpose." That purpose is to glorify You and make

Your name known through the love I share with others in Your name. Joy and peace come as a result of seeking unity and living in a spirit of oneness. They don't come before it. Let me walk in faith by seeking oneness so that I can also experience the fruit of that oneness in my own spirit. In Christ's name and by His authority, I pray this.

Take Up the Helmet of Salvation

Father, salvation should produce fruit in my life and in the lives of others who place their trust in Christ. The fruit of unity and oneness comes to light in the account of the early church members who were saved. It says in Acts 4:32, "The congregation of those who believed were of one heart and soul; and not one of them claimed that anything belonging to him was his own, but all things were common property to them." I pray that my salvation will produce the fruit of unity in all I do and that I will view all I am with the perspective of how I can bring good to others in Your name and for Your glory. In Christ's name and by His authority, I pray this.

Take Up the Sword of the Spirit

It is written in John 17:23, "I in them and You in Me, that they may be perfected in unity, so that the world may know that You sent Me, and loved them, even as You have loved Me." Jesus told us plainly throughout His time on earth that unity lets others know we are followers of the one true God. He prayed for our unity. Let His words and His prayer be made manifest not only in my life but in the lives of my family members, fellow church members, and believers across our nation and around the world. Your Word says in Romans 15:5 that You grant unity: "May the

God who gives perseverance and encouragement grant you to be of the same mind with one another according to Christ Jesus." I ask for You to grant this same mind to all of us. In Christ's name and by His authority, I pray this.

2

ACCEPTING ALL

*He Himself is our peace, who made both groups into one and
broke down the barrier of the dividing wall, by abolishing
in His flesh the enmity, which is the Law of commandments
contained in ordinances, so that in Himself He might make
the two into one new man, thus establishing peace.*

EPHESIANS 2:14-15

The story is told of an elderly woman who visited a local church one day. When the service drew to a close, this woman in her worn and tattered clothes went forward in order to become a member. The preacher listened to her as she told him that she believed in Christ and wanted to be baptized. He also found out that she was still and had been a cleaning woman all her life.

The preacher thought, *She is so disheveled, and she even has a foul odor about her. She cleans toilets for a living—what would the members think of her?* He told her that she needed to go home and pray about it for a while before she was baptized. The next week, she came forward again during the invitation. She told the preacher that she had prayed about it and still wanted to be baptized. But the preacher told her to go home and pray some more.

A few weeks later the preacher ran across the elderly woman while out doing some errands. He asked her why she hadn't been at church for a while. "Is everything all right?"

"Oh, yes," she said. "I talked with Jesus, and He told me not to worry about becoming a member of your church."

"He did?" asked the preacher, a little taken aback.

"Oh, yes," she replied. "Jesus said even He hasn't been able to get into your church, and He's been trying for years."

Precious few of us ever fully live up to others' expectations. The story of the cleaning lady is extreme and meant to be funny, but the truth is that our differences often divide us, whether they are based on preference or diversity. Each of us who comprise the body of Christ has a unique background that comes with unique preferences and idiosyncrasies in our personalities. This diversity brings a greater variety and strength to the body of Christ as a whole—but it often divides us as well.

In His family, God has brought together people who have a variety of likes and dislikes, interests, dreams, and baggage and asked us all not only to get along, but also to love one another. We read of this in Galatians: "There is neither Jew nor Greek, there is neither slave nor free man, there is neither male nor female; for you are all one in Christ Jesus" (3:28). Even though we came as Jew, Greek, slave, free, male, or female, in Christ, we have been joined together as "one new man" (Ephesians 2:15).

Despite our different backgrounds, histories, and preferences, God has asked us to live, love, worship, and work together while operating in unity as part of the family of God. In order to do that, we must embrace Paul's admonition to "accept one another, just as Christ also accepted us to the glory of God" (Romans 15:7). And we must do more than simply recite this verse. The many rifts among us reveal that precious few of us have put flesh on these words.

We are called as brothers and sisters in Christ to accept one another just as Christ accepted us. Accepting one another is critical to our ability to celebrate and enjoy the freedom that we have in the Lord. It is one of the first steps we must take in order to overcome our divisions. Paul didn't say we have to *agree* with one another. He said we have to *accept* one another. Yes, even those whom we do not like or prefer.

Keep in mind, God has not asked us to accept all behaviors. Sin is sin, and we are to oppose it and not associate with sinful situations. However, we have been called to love and accept all people as fellow human beings made in the divine image of God.

Much of our division and infighting occurs due to differences in personal values, opinions, and preferences. But each of us has been gifted a free will by God to live life's journey. To divide over this gift is a shame. Likewise, to deny someone else his or her freedom to live in this gift is hypocritical. Unity begins with acceptance. It starts with allowing each person to be personally responsible for themselves and accountable to God—not to you.

Put On the Belt of Truth

> Father, when I choose to judge someone else, I am deciding on division. Give me the grace I need in order to refrain from judging others, leaving room for You to do all You need to do. I know You have not called me to accept all behaviors. You have standards and truth. But You have also asked me not to judge others. Your truth is clear in Matthew 7:1-5, and I stand in this truth: "Do not judge so that you will not be judged. For in the way you judge, you will be judged; and by your standard of measure, it will be measured to you. Why do you look at the speck that is in your brother's eye, but do not notice the log that is in your own eye? Or how can you say to your brother, 'Let me take the speck out of your eye,' and behold, the log is in your own eye? You

hypocrite, first take the log out of your own eye, and then you will see clearly to take the speck out of your brother's eye." May my life reflect the fact that I wear this belt of truth. In Christ's name and by His authority, I pray this.

Put On the Breastplate of Righteousness

Lord, with the breastplate of righteousness I stand against any faulty, untrue, dividing belief system created by mankind. Rather, I look to You, Jesus, as the model of true righteousness. You have shown us in Your Word, as recorded in Matthew 9:12-13, "It is not those who are healthy who need a physician, but those who are sick. But go and learn what this means: 'I desire compassion, and not sacrifice,' for I did not come to call the righteous, but sinners." Jesus, let my righteousness model Your righteousness, because You have demonstrated what real unity and authentic love and acceptance look like. With that level of righteousness, division will have to dissolve into oneness. In Christ's name and by His authority, I pray this.

Put On the Shoes of Peace

Father, I put on the shoes of peace as I wrestle with the lack of peace created by division. Let me start with myself and be sure that my footsteps are ones of peace as I walk among everyone I meet. When a thought of judgment, blame, or even condescension comes upon my spirit, convict me quickly and make me aware so that I can adjust to Your standard of peace and acceptance. Make me an instrument of acceptance that encourages others. In Christ's name and by His authority, I pray this.

Take Up the Shield of Faith

Lord, a lack of acceptance often arises out of a heart filled with fear, doubt, and envy. It is a defense mechanism we use in seeking to protect ourselves. But the shield of faith reminds me of Your truth written in Romans 8:31, which says, "If God is for us, who is against us?" When someone comes against me in any way, help me remember that the true issue is not the person seeking division, but rather the tactics of Satan. The person is not my enemy, and unity is the cure to any divide erected around me. Help me not to fall into Satan's trap of comparison. As it is written in Romans 14:1, "Accept the one who is weak in faith, but not for the purpose of passing judgment on his opinions." I am accountable to You for my faith, as each person is. Let my thoughts, words, and actions reflect a high level of faith in my heart. In Christ's name and by His authority, I pray this.

Take Up the Helmet of Salvation

Father, I put on the helmet of my salvation as I deal with the destructive level of judgment and division raising its ugly head in my own life, my church, my workplace, my community, my nation, and our world. We are all accepted in Christ Jesus by the power and authority of His sacrifice, whether we acknowledge and receive that acceptance or not. It is there to be received through faith. Forgive me for standing in the way of anyone receiving Christ's acceptance because I have offended him or her with my own judgment, modeling a wrong perspective. Let the helmet of salvation based on Your Word be ever present in my thinking, as it is written in

1 Timothy 1:15, "It is a trustworthy statement, deserving full acceptance, that Christ Jesus came into the world to save sinners, among whom I am foremost of all." In Christ's name and by His authority, I pray this.

Take Up the Sword of the Spirit

Lord, help me learn and study Your Word at such a level that it becomes hidden in my heart so that I might not sin against You, as it says in Psalm 119:11. Motivate me to use the list at the end of this book in order to familiarize myself with Scriptures related to unity and oneness. Help my mind be healthy and receptive to Your Word so that Your truth can take root in my life and then flow outward to others. The sword of the Spirit is only as sharp as the Word I have from You within me, the Scriptures I am willing to use and apply. Help all of us in Your collective body both learn and apply the truth of Your Word and not settle for entertainment, stories, and tickled ears. Raise up leaders who know Your Word, study Your Word, practice Your Word, and teach Your Word to Your flock. In Christ's name and by His authority, I pray this.

3

HUMBLE HEARTS

I, the prisoner of the Lord, implore you to walk in a manner worthy of the calling with which you have been called, with all humility and gentleness, with patience, showing tolerance for one another in love.

EPHESIANS 4:1-2

don't know about you, but I really enjoy the commercials that show professional football players being brought face-to-face with their mothers. Big, strong players who can run over people, block people, knock people down, and are muscular and powerful suddenly become meek in the presence of their mom. As a former chaplain for the Dallas Cowboys, I got to see the transformation in person, watching grown men become kids again when their mom came to practice or a game.

When my own mother was still alive, I couldn't get away with anything in her house. If I even started to disagree with her on something, she'd quickly remind me who was in charge.

Meekness isn't weakness. Meekness recognizes who is in charge. And for those of us who grew up with strong mothers, we always knew who was in charge.

Unfortunately, we rarely see meekness today in the collective character of our culture. Rather, pride and arrogance open the door for people to act and speak in ways that are filled with disrespect, dishonor, and disunity. The political realm is just one area where this attitude shows up. Pride drives wedges in relationships, groups, political parties, families, churches, and even nations.

Jesus spoke against pride by telling us that we would be blessed if we choose not to live with this spirit that led to Satan's demise. Jesus said in Matthew 5:5, "Blessed are the gentle, for they shall inherit the earth." The Greek word *praÿs*—translated as "gentle" in this Scripture—means "mild" or "humble." Of all the statements Jesus made in His Sermon on the Mount, this one had to astonish His audience the most. After all, the people around Him were looking to Him to lead. They sought someone who was strong and could deliver them from Rome. The concept of strength in meekness runs contrary to our earthly mind-set.

But being meek or humble does not mean being wishy-washy. It does not mean being indecisive. Nor does it mean getting walked on by others. Rather, meekness refers to strength under control.

Think of a wild horse being broken. As the cowboy or cowgirl rides the powerful animal, they are not seeking to reduce its power. Instead, they are seeking to train the horse to control its power in a productive way.

When we choose to live in ways that are displeasing to the Lord—ways that encourage and breed division in our relationships, churches, and nation—we are using our strength wrong. We are failing to restrain the power God has given us and funnel it in productive ways.

Pride always leads to destruction. If a horse chooses not to allow the rider to steer him and bucks off the rider, disunity occurs. Similarly, when believers claim that it is our right to say whatever we want to whomever we want—when we insult, criticize, poke fun at, bully, isolate, or ignore others simply because we do not agree with them on nonessential issues or policies—we directly contribute to division.

Humility ought to be our response to grasping our identity under God. When we allow His will and His kingdom directives to govern our thoughts, words, and actions, then unity will be the result. Because God is a God of unity. It is only when we allow our own pride to usurp His rightful place in our hearts and minds that disunity is allowed to thrive.

Put On the Belt of Truth

Father, Proverbs 11:2 tells us, "When pride comes, then comes dishonor, but with the humble is wisdom." Humility creates a heart of wisdom within us, but we limit that wisdom when we surrender to pride. Not only does pride lead to dishonoring ourselves, but also to dishonoring others. Your Word says in Proverbs 29:23, "A man's pride will bring him low, but a humble spirit will obtain honor." In order to honor ourselves as those made in Your image, we must start with a spirit of humility. Then that honor will extend beyond us to others in a spirit of unity. Let Your truth resonate in my spirit, and also in the spirits of others. In Christ's name and by His authority, I pray this.

Put On the Breastplate of Righteousness

Father, Your Word tells us to walk in holiness and righteousness. The root of this righteousness rests in Jesus Christ. We are to seek to model Him in all we do. Jesus modeled sacrificing everything for the highest good of all involved. Philippians 2:8 says, "Being found in appearance as a man, He humbled Himself by becoming obedient to the point of death, even death on a cross." Make my heart righteous that I may be a person after Christ's own heart. I pray I will embody wisdom and understanding through all I do and say, as it is written in James 3:13, "Who among you is wise and understanding? Let him show by his good behavior his deeds in the gentleness of wisdom." In Christ's name and by His authority, I pray this.

Put On the Shoes of Peace

Lord, one of the evidences of not living a Spirit-filled life is disunity, as Galatians 5:19-20 points out. You have given me the Holy Spirit so that I can have the power and authority to remove the roots of disunity from my own heart, in an attitude of humility and surrender. By embracing Your call to pursue peace with all people, given in Hebrews 12:14, I can help create an atmosphere where oneness thrives. Make my words be full of peace, undergirded with humility. Surround me with Your Spirit so that I am continually walking the pathway of peace. Help me "seek peace and pursue it," according to Your Word in Psalm 34:14. In Christ's name and by His authority, I pray this.

Take Up the Shield of Faith

God, it is in times of pride or in those moments when I feel I need to defend myself that humility disappears. This breeds a spirit of disunity because I am only focused on myself and my own preservation. But You have asked me to live according to the truth, based on faith in Your Word. Your Word says that I do not need to defend myself. Your Word says that You watch over me and care for me. Second Thessalonians 3:3 reminds me of this: "The Lord is faithful, and He will strengthen and protect you from the evil one." May I live with full faith in this truth so that I will not let the pursuit of personal protection become an opening for division to rise in my own heart. In Christ's name and by His authority, I pray this.

Take Up the Helmet of Salvation

Lord, the security that comes from Your salvation sets me free to release pride and live in a spirit of humility. Your salvation covers me not only in eternity but also while I live on earth. Help me look to You when I feel insecure so I do not give the enemy an opportunity to increase pride in my heart. Your Word says in Psalm 138:7, "Though I walk in the midst of trouble, You will revive me; You will stretch forth Your hand against the wrath of my enemies, and Your right hand will save me." Your right hand is my salvation. I do not need to exalt myself over anyone else or look down upon someone in order to feel secure. It is in honoring others that I will walk more fully in the salvation You have provided for me because, in doing so, I am living in alignment under Your rule. In Christ's name and by His authority, I pray this.

Take Up the Sword of the Spirit

Lord, as I take hold of the sword of the Spirit in every moment of my life, give me wisdom through Your Word to align my thoughts, words, and actions under You. When I find it difficult to humble myself, Lord, direct me to the Scripture that reveals what I need to know in order to guide me into a spirit of humility. Protect me from the enemy's attempts to distort or twist Your Word as he did with Eve in the garden. Guard my mind so that Your truth resonates within me. Help me counter Satan's lies with Your Word by saying, "It is written," and then repeating the truth of Scripture. Reveal to me where I have been deceived by the enemy and show me Your truth to counter those lies. In Christ's name and by His authority, I pray this.

4

PERSONAL HOLINESS

Where jealousy and selfish ambition exist, there
is disorder and every evil thing.

JAMES 3:16

At salvation, God deposited within each of us a new nature—that is our spirit. The spirit contains all of God's power, presence, joy, peace, righteousness, and holiness. Everything God has in store for you resides in the new spirit within you, and it is perfect. It is holy. Your new spirit, which hosts the divine nature of God planted in you, is the only place to which the spiritual realm of darkness does not have access. The problem is that your perfect spirit is lodged within your imperfect soul.

Your soul—mind, will, and emotions—is affected by so many different and changing variables that you can find yourself acting one way one year and another way another year. Your personality can be up one day and down the next because your soul is telling your body what to do.

Everyone has a distorted soul. You are not unique in that regard. Some people's souls are more distorted than others, but everyone is viewing life through the lens of a distorted soul. Our bodies do wrong things because they're following the direction of our distorted souls. This is an important point to realize: You can't fix you.

Personal holiness comes through the expansion of the seed of the perfect Spirit placed within you. It is not about you seeking to keep a list of dos and don'ts. Holiness comes through abiding with Christ and His Word at such a level that His Spirit grows within you in order to dominate your mind, body, and soul.

Here is how it works. The Holy Spirit releases the truths, the essence, the presence of God—what you might call the "DNA" of God—into your human spirit. Your spirit then delivers it to your soul. Yet we're not experiencing this release in our lives to a greater degree because in order for the soul to grab on to and receive the things of the spirit, it must agree with the spirit. However, most of our souls are so filled with deception and distortion, the spirit isn't free to release its power into us. Therefore, you must start by replacing the distortions within you with the truth—placing the truth of God inside you—because the truth is the only thing that the spirit and soul can agree upon.

The only way to experience true personal holiness is to submit your mind, will, and emotions—your soul—to the overarching truth of God. Living a life of holiness is a foundational part of living in unity with others. When we lack personal holiness, divisions will inevitably arise, as we read in James 3:16, "Where jealousy and selfish ambition exist, there is disorder and every evil thing."

We cannot force unity. But we can encourage it by seeking to live according to God's Word and His call to personal holiness.

Put On the Belt of Truth

> Lord, Your Word calls us to a life of holiness. We are to perfect it over time through surrender to You. We read of Your truth in 2 Corinthians 7:1, which says, "Let us

cleanse ourselves from all defilement of flesh and spirit, perfecting holiness in the fear of God." I want to cleanse myself from all such defilement. I ask You to help me and all of us in the corporate body of Christ, that we may perfect holiness out of a heart of gratitude and reverence for You. Will You help us live in this truth? Your Word is truth, as John 17:17 says. So many people today talk about "my truth," but there is only one truth—Your Word. Until we align ourselves under Your Word, we are not walking in truth. Help us do this so that we may truly understand what it means to live a life of holiness. In Christ's name and by His authority, I pray this.

Put On the Breastplate of Righteousness

Father, You have asked me to be holy. Holiness is an embodiment of Your righteousness. Your Word states in 1 Peter 1:13-16, "Prepare your minds for action, keep sober in spirit, fix your hope completely on the grace to be brought to you at the revelation of Jesus Christ. As obedient children, do not be conformed to the former lusts which were yours in your ignorance, but like the Holy One who called you, be holy yourselves also in all your behavior; because it is written, 'You shall be holy, for I am holy.'" Help me prepare my mind for action by remaining sober in spirit and fixing my hope entirely on the grace that will come to me at the revelation of Jesus. Help us in the corporate body of Christ not to be conformed to the world and its passions. Give us wisdom to know what holiness looks and feels like. Convict us of any unholiness so we can repent. Help us not judge one another but rather allow You room to judge each of us individually in our own hearts. Draw us to repentance so that we can be set free to live a life of righteousness, which will lead to an atmosphere of unity in our relationships, work, church, and nation. In Christ's name and by His authority, I pray this.

Put On the Shoes of Peace

Lord, walking in the shoes of peace comes through personal holiness. We cannot look at the world around us and question the lack of peace when we choose to embrace lives that lack personal holiness. It starts with each of us surrendering to You. Hebrews 12:14 states it as clearly as possible: "Make every effort to live in peace with everyone and to be holy; without holiness no one will see the Lord" (NIV). You have asked that we "be holy" because it is part of our spiritual warfare strategy. Help me remember this, and help us all look inward and let go of our judgment of other people, even when we disagree with them. In Christ's name and by His authority, I pray this.

Take Up the Shield of Faith

God, Satan likes to send darts of doubt into our lives in order to breed thoughts of shame in us. This shame can cause us to believe that we could never be holy. It can cause us to give up even trying, since we remember our struggles and sins so well. But Your call to holiness is manifested by Your Spirit's power in us. It is not a result of our own human effort. If we could be perfect on our own, then there would have been no need for Jesus' death and resurrection. But because of His sacrifice, Your Word reminds us to take up the shield of faith against Satan's accusations. Romans 8:1 says, "There is now no condemnation for those who are in Christ Jesus." I rest behind this shield in faith, calling upon the holiness of Jesus Himself to be transferred to my humanity, that I may be called the righteousness of God, as 2 Corinthians 5:21 says. In Christ's name and by His authority, I pray this.

Take Up the Helmet of Salvation

Lord, the salvation I have due to Jesus' sacrifice for my sins gives me the freedom to approach You boldly through prayer. I come to Your throne knowing that when You look at me, You see His righteousness. It is in gratitude for the helmet of salvation, which Christ has supplied, that I can then live according to Your will and ways. Gratitude is to be my motivation. May it be our motivation as a church body. May gratitude draw us together in unity as we remember that none of us is perfect. May we show grace to others in their imperfections because the same salvation Christ has given to us has also been given to others. In Christ's name and by His authority, I pray this.

Take Up the Sword of the Spirit

Lord, may I live with the full power of the sword of the Spirit. May all Your kingdom followers study Your Word, know Your Word, practice Your Word, and speak Your Word. Your Word is the sword of the Spirit. Let the truth of this sink into our hearts more fully. Let our personal holiness come about as a result of the growth of Your Word in us through the seed You have planted. Philippians 2:5 tells us, "In your relationships with one another, have the same mindset as Christ Jesus" (NIV). We have Christ's mind-set when we abide in Your Word, the sword of the Spirit. Let this be the theme of our churches worldwide. May our pastors preach and teach Your Word so that we may learn more. May we also as individuals take personal responsibility to study Your Word and adapt it as our mind-set. In Christ's name and by His authority, I pray this.

5

CORPORATE REPENTANCE FOR DISUNITY

If I shut up the heavens so that there is no rain, or if I command the
locust to devour the land, or if I send pestilence among My people,
and My people who are called by My name humble themselves and
pray and seek My face and turn from their wicked ways, then I will
hear from heaven, will forgive their sin and will heal their land.

2 Chronicles 7:13-14

Repentance is widely misunderstood in Christian circles today. Many people feel as if repentance only involves saying you are sorry. That is not the case. Repentance also includes a complete change of mind-set about that of which you are repenting.

With our focus on oneness in this book, we need to corporately repent of disunity. We need not only to say we are sorry for the disunity in our churches and country, but also to change our minds and recognize the sin as God views it. We cannot call out someone else for causing disunity only to fall into the trap of creating disunity ourselves through anger, hateful words, or dishonoring behavior.

The issue many people face in our nation is that they may offer an apology, but they don't turn from the sin and then turn toward God. This is important to realize. You can turn away from sin and still be miserable, living in the consequences of that sin and leaving an open door for Satan to reintroduce the sin. It is only when you turn toward God with a broken spirit in order to reestablish fellowship with Him and reconciliation with others that true repentance takes place—canceling, reversing, and mitigating the repercussions of your sin.

For example, if you were driving the wrong direction on the highway and you realized what you were doing wrong, you would exit the highway. But if you only exited the highway and did not start driving in the right direction, you would be no better off than you were before. You have turned from the wrong way, but you have not turned toward the right way.

The corporate body of Christ needs not only to repent of our disunity—and, on behalf of our nation, the disunity that thrives in our land—but also to turn toward unity in active steps, words, and thoughts. God's Word is clear:

> If I shut up the heavens so that there is no rain, or if I command the locust to devour the land, or if I send pestilence among My people, and My people who are called by My name humble themselves and pray and seek My face and turn from their wicked ways, then I will hear from heaven, will forgive their sin and will heal their land. Now My eyes will be open and My ears attentive to the prayer offered in this place (2 Chronicles 7:13-15).

We must turn from disunity while simultaneously seeking God's face and His heart of unity. When we do that, we will experience the power of His healing, life, and peace in the body of Christ, which will then overflow to our land.

Put On the Belt of Truth

Lord, You have not called the righteous to repentance,

but rather sinners (Luke 5:32). This truth is where we must start. If we look outwardly and accuse others of being disunified while ignoring our own complacency, complicity, or active engagement with disunity, we will not be contributing to unity in our land. We must begin by confessing our own sins, and then confess the sins of our people. Isaiah modeled this for us when You revealed his sinfulness to him. He first acknowledged his own sin and ruin before moving on to that of others. He said, "Woe is me, for I am ruined! Because I am a man of unclean lips, and I live among a people of unclean lips; for my eyes have seen the King, the LORD of hosts" (Isaiah 6:5). Thank You for revealing this truth to me as I pray. In Christ's name and by His authority, I pray this.

Put On the Breastplate of Righteousness

Father, disunity has left a crimson stain on our nation and the collective church body. Its origins stretch back to the beginning of time. I seek Your righteousness, which comes to us through the shed blood of Jesus Christ. Let Your righteousness cover our sins so that we may find Your grace, mercy, and healing from the consequences of what we have done. In Christ's name and by His authority, I pray this.

Put On the Shoes of Peace

Lord, make peace the borders of our homes, churches, communities, and nation, as is noted in Psalm 147:14. I come to You in repentance on behalf of myself and all of us who call on Your name for the disunity we have allowed among ourselves. I also repent of our silence, the times we have not spoken up for unity when we were given the opportunity to do so. Unity spreads peace. Forgive us for walking in the shoes of division, hatred, spite, arrogance, and animosity. In Christ's name and by His authority, I pray this.

Take Up the Shield of Faith

God, thank You for the shield I can take up by believing in Your Word, which clearly says in 1 John 1:9 that if we confess our sins, You are faithful and just to forgive us our sins. I hold up this shield against all the consequences brought into our lives, families, churches, communities, and nation due to the sin of division. I hold up the shield of faith knowing that You are faithful and can reverse whatever damage has been done. Not only that, but I also know You can restore the years the locusts have stolen, as Joel 2:25 says. In Christ's name and by His authority, I pray this.

Take Up the Helmet of Salvation

Lord, thank You that our victory over the sin of disunity is secure due to the full payment and sacrifice of the blood of the Lamb. Jesus, Your willingness to humble Yourself in order to be made our sacrifice gives us the assurance that we can repent of our sins and be heard. I ask that You would strengthen our feelings of security and our faith in Your salvation so that we, as the body of Christ, will pray more boldly concerning the repentance of our sins. In Christ's name and by His authority, I pray this.

Take Up the Sword of the Spirit

Lord, I take up the sword of the Spirit, Your Word,

and pray Nehemiah's prayer in Nehemiah 1:5-6
on behalf of my own nation: "I beseech You, O LORD
God of heaven, the great and awesome God, who
preserves the covenant and lovingkindness for those
who love Him and keep His commandments, let Your
ear now be attentive and Your eyes open to hear the
prayer of Your servant which I am praying before
You now, day and night, on behalf of the sons of
Israel Your servants, confessing the sins of the sons of
Israel which we have sinned against You." In Christ's
name and by His authority, I pray this for myself, my
people, the collective church body, and my nation.

6

MUTUAL SERVICE

You were called to freedom, brethren; only do not
turn your freedom into an opportunity
for the flesh, but through love serve one another.

GALATIANS 5:13

Service is the true path to unity. Mutual service opens the funnel of engagement with God because when we serve each other, He recognizes kingdom qualities and virtues in us. If we want to have a greater manifestation of God's unity in our relationships, home, work, community, and nation, then our thoughts, words, and interactions must be characterized by a servant's heart.

If we are to develop a servant's heart, we must first discover what the word *service* means in a biblical context. To serve is to focus on others and act for their benefit in the name of Christ. Service begins with a humble attitude and involves actively looking out for the interests of others. You become a true servant when you come alongside others in unity and help them improve spiritually, physically, emotionally, or circumstantially. You serve when your words or actions make someone else's life better.

God calls us to a life of humility and service because these two things promote the bond of peace and unity, overpowering any disunified forces we may face. In order to live out God's desire for us, we need to surrender our wants, schedules, and expectations to Him so we can meet other people's needs. In doing so, we will bring glory to God while strengthening our own spiritual walk and simultaneously encouraging unity in our spheres of influence.

God rewards service through His unifying presence among His followers. But He will also reward it in your personal life. Just as a waiter or waitress will receive a greater tip for excellent service, our Lord notices what you do for others. Your service will be rewarded here on earth or in heaven (Ephesians 6:7-8; Colossians 3:23-24).

So what does servanthood look like? The greatest story of servanthood, outside of the cross, is set in a roomful of men with dirty feet. Shortly before Christ went to the cross, He gave us a living example of service.

> Jesus, knowing that the Father had given all things into His hands, and that He had come forth from God and was going back to God, got up from supper, and laid aside His garments; and taking a towel, He girded Himself.
>
> Then He poured water into the basin, and began to wash the disciples' feet and to wipe them with the towel with which He was girded (John 13:3-5).

Just as He had done throughout His earthly ministry, the Master became the slave. The Maker became the servant. Jesus donned a towel, grabbed a bucket, and washed the feet of those who, in just a few hours, would desert Him. To His very last day on earth, Jesus passionately and compassionately pursued unity among those with whom He shared space. And He did this through a heart of service, grace, and love.

Put On the Belt of Truth

Father, Your Word says in 1 Peter 4:10, "As each one has received a special gift, employ it in serving one another as good stewards of the manifold grace of God." We are to live by Your truth. That means that we must do everything we can to serve each other. This enables us to be good stewards of Your manifold grace. Lord, I do not want Your grace to go to waste on me because I chose not to steward it wisely. Help me serve others. Help all of us in Your body to enter into mutual service so no one is lacking and we are all promoting the benefits of unity locally and nationally. In Christ's name and by His authority, I pray this.

Put On the Breastplate of Righteousness

Lord, make me a person who serves gladly. Your Word tells me to do this in Romans 12:9-11, which says, "Let love be without hypocrisy. Abhor what is evil; cling to what is good. Be devoted to one another in brotherly love; give preference to one another in honor; not lagging behind in diligence, fervent in spirit, serving the Lord." In serving You I am also to serve others. Open the eyes of my heart, Lord, so I can understand this high calling. Help me and all of us in the body of Christ be devoted to one another in brotherly love, giving preference to one another. When we do this and walk according to Your prescribed righteousness for our lives, we will experience the unity we have been placed here on earth to model to those around us. In Christ's name and by His authority, I pray this.

Put On the Shoes of Peace

Today, Lord, I choose to wear the shoes of peace. When
I feel offended by someone—no matter how harshly
they treat me—let me remember whose shoes I am
walking in: Yours. Let each of us remember that we
are made in Your image and that our steps are to be
steps of peace. Help all of us in my family, workplace,
community, church, and nation not to react according
to our emotions but rather maintain peace by showing
compassion, empathy, kindness, gentleness, and love to
all others. Let us deflect attacks through kindness so they
do not escalate. This will provide greater opportunities for
service. In Christ's name and by His authority, I pray this.

Take Up the Shield of Faith

Father, I need to take up the shield of faith when my
feelings are hurt because it is that shield which will give
me the ability to respond correctly, in grace. Serving
those whom I love is easy. Serving those with whom
I experience division is hard. I want to represent You
by being a servant to those whose personalities and
preferences do not naturally align with mine. Let me model
unity through my service. Let us in the body of Christ
model unity by serving others with hearts of goodness,
grace, kindness, and encouragement. We can do this
when we use the shield of faith as a deterrent for the
enemy's darts aimed at us, attempting to provoke us to
division. In Christ's name and by His authority, I pray this.

Take Up the Helmet of Salvation

Lord, on the cross Christ secured the abundant life for

us—both in the here and now and in the future. This
gift of salvation is to be the motivation for our unified,
collective, and mutual service. It is the heart that drives
the hands, the mind-set that drives the movements. Paul
said we were called to freedom in Galatians 5:13. Yet
we are not to use that freedom as an opportunity for the
flesh, but instead as empowerment to serve one another
in love. Far too many of us have forgotten the freedom
the cross has secured, so we lack the impetus and
motivation to serve. Forgive us. Have mercy on us. Some
of us are still bound in legalism, not feeling the full effect
of Christ's atonement in our lives, so service feels like an
additional burden. Free us. Release us from those lies.
Help me and those for whom I am praying fully grasp and
appropriate the freedom that Jesus Christ has purchased
on our behalf so we will tap into the true spirit of unity in
service. In Christ's name and by His authority, I pray this.

Take Up the Sword of the Spirit

Lord, I'm available. Create in me the desire to do the
works You have in mind for me. Let me see more of Your
plan for me each day. I believe You will give me the
desire to do Your will and the ability to pull it off. It is
written in Philippians 2:12-13, "Work out your salvation
with fear and trembling; for it is God who is at work in
you, both to will and to work for His good pleasure." I
am on assignment for You, so give me the desire to
obey and the ability to carry out Your plan for me. Help
me be obedient and listen for Your voice. I am custom-
made for the service You have for me. Isaiah 44:2
says, "The LORD who made you and formed you from
the womb...will help you." I give You the credit for my

design, my purpose, and the service I am to do in Your name. For it is written in Psalm 138:8, "The LORD will accomplish what concerns me." You have made me with a purpose, and You are determined to fulfill it. I know that purpose involves unity and oneness, because Jesus said that is how we reflect Him and You. Make me a vessel ready for service and use me to spread oneness. In Christ's name and by His authority, I pray this.

7

EMBRACING DIVERSITY

Being diligent to preserve the unity of the Spirit in the bond of peace.

Ephesians 4:3

Unity is not uniformity, nor is it sameness. Just as the Godhead is made up of three distinct Persons—the Father, the Son, and the Holy Spirit—each unique in personhood and yet at the same time one in essence, unity reflects a oneness that does not negate individuality. Unity does not mean everyone needs to be like everyone else. God's creative variety is replete, displaying itself through a humanity crafted in different shapes, colors, and styles. Each of us, in one form or another, is unique.

Unity occurs when we combine our unique differences together as we head toward a common goal. It is the sense that the thing that we are gathered for and moving toward is bigger than our own individual preferences.

Through the establishment of the church along with His overarching rulership above it, God has created a reflection of His kingdom in heaven on earth. He has reconciled racially divided groups into "one new man" (Ephesians 2:14-15), uniting them into a new body (verse 16) so the church can function in unity (4:13). The church is the place where racial, gender, and class distinctions are no longer to be divisive because of our unity in Christ (Galatians 3:28). This does not negate differences that remain intact—oneness simply means that those differences are embraced. Joining our unique strengths together, we add strength to strength, making a completer and more balanced whole based on our mutual relationship with and commitment to Christ.

So important is the issue of oneness in the church that we are told to look out for people who seek to undermine it (Romans 16:17). In fact, God promised to judge those who divide His church (1 Corinthians 3:17). This is because the church is to reflect the values of the kingdom of God to a world in desperate need of experiencing Him. The church is the only authentic cross-racial, cross-cultural, and cross-generational basis for oneness in existence. It is the only institution on earth obligated to live under God's authority while enabled to do so through His Spirit.

Ephesians 4:3 says that we are to "preserve the unity of the Spirit." Scripture uses the term *preserve*, indicating that we don't create unity. Authentic unity, then, cannot be mandated or manufactured. This is so because God desires that His standards alone serve as the basis, criteria, and foundation for oneness. It is also why He thwarts attempts at unity that ignore or exclude Him (Genesis 11:1-9). The Spirit created unity when we were saved. Our job is to find out what the Spirit has already done so we can live, walk in, and embrace that reality.

Put On the Belt of Truth

> Lord, the foundation of our unity is not found in our sameness. To be unified does not mean we talk the same, dress the same, have the same interests, or take the same approach to how we solve issues in life. Unity is working together toward a shared goal under You. The truth of Your Word must guide our hearts and

minds in order for us to overcome division. It says in
Ephesians 2:14-16, "He Himself is our peace, who
made both groups into one and broke down the barrier
of the dividing wall, by abolishing in His flesh the
enmity, which is the Law of commandments contained
in ordinances, so that in Himself He might make the
two into one new man, thus establishing peace, and
might reconcile them both in one body to God through
the cross, by it having put to death the enmity." The truth
is that our dividing walls have already been broken
down by Christ Himself. He makes us one. Our unity
already exists. We only need to access it by aligning
with one another under the overarching rule of love You
have given to us in the two greatest commandments,
outlined in Matthew 22:37-39. I pray this truth will be
made manifest throughout our nation and around the
world. In Christ's name and by His authority, I pray this.

Put On the Breastplate of Righteousness

Father, Your Word tells us that we are one in You. I seek
to take up the breastplate of righteousness by identifying
myself first as a kingdom disciple under You. Galatians
3:28 reminds me, "There is neither Jew nor Greek, there
is neither slave nor free man, there is neither male nor
female; for you are all one in Christ Jesus." This does not
mean I have to give up my heritage or ethnicity, gender
or preferences. It means that these things no longer
govern my choices. I can exercise free will to choose
love and unity with anyone and everyone. What society
has divided and continues to divide through all the hate
speech circulating today does not need to have authority
over me, because Jesus has cut through the rhetoric,

making us all one—if we learn how to embrace it. Make this a righteous reality not only in my own life but also in the lives of my loved ones, church, coworkers, and fellow citizens. In Christ's name and by His authority, I pray this.

Put On the Shoes of Peace

Lord, peace seems so distant from our everyday lives. Offense over our divisions creeps up seemingly everywhere. To stand firm in the shoes of peace means I must be willing to embrace the diversity of those who think they are divided from me. They simply do not know yet that we are truly one in You. Open their eyes so they will also know this truth. But until their eyes are open, give me the courage and self-awareness to actively embrace diversity around me rather than distance myself from it. Let me be a model of peace, showing that oneness overpowers division while simultaneously promoting peace. In Christ's name and by His authority, I pray this.

Take Up the Shield of Faith

Lord, I lift up my family, coworkers, neighbors, church, community, nation, and world to You today, asking that You be our shield, defending us from the attacks of the enemy intended to divide us. Help us trust Your plan for unity as outlined for us in John 17. Let the words that Jesus spoke resonate so strongly within us that we cannot help but hear them and abide by them. Give us opportunities to celebrate diversity without negating our own uniqueness and strength. Show us how joining together promotes the greater good for all involved. In Christ's name and by His authority, I pray this.

Take Up the Helmet of Salvation

Father, You know the lies the enemy has spoken over humanity. Distance, division, hate speech, judgment, and fear reign. This is because we have taken off the helmet of salvation, which would block those lies from reaching our minds and thoughts. Cover me, and cover all of us who are seeking You, with the protective authority of the blood of Jesus Christ, which was purchased for us through His death and resurrection. Create a protective bubble around our thoughts so that we do not view each other as enemies. Rather, lift our blinders so we can identify who the enemy truly is—Satan himself. When we recognize this, we will intentionally seek ways to encourage diversity and uniqueness, rather than fall prey to the traps of comparison, jealousy, envy, and hate that the enemy has planted in our hearts and minds. Life is not a competition. It is a journey. Give me and all of us the wisdom to journey in a spirit of oneness, always caring for the greater good. In Christ's name and by His authority, I pray this.

Take Up the Sword of the Spirit

Father, as You know, Satan spends most of his time trying to divide the body of Christ because he knows that Your power and glory are both accessed and magnified through unity. When we embrace and celebrate our differences, we reflect the manifold greatness of Your image. Satan is not spending his time trying to make the world wicked, because he doesn't have to help the world become wicked. We are all born in wickedness and division. Satan just lets the world do its natural thing, and individuals divide, fight, and oppress each other. But if Satan can keep us as Christians ineffective due to a lack of cooperation and mutual edification, he will prevent us from modeling the diverse but unified kingdom of God as an alternative to the world's chaos. Your kingdom is diverse. As it is written in Revelation 7:9, "After these things I looked, and behold, a great multitude which no one could count, from every nation and all tribes and peoples and tongues, standing before the throne and before the Lamb, clothed in white robes, and palm branches were in their hands." May it be done on earth as it is in heaven. In Christ's name and by His authority, I pray this.

8

SPEAKING LIFE

The tongue has the power of life and death,
and those who love it will eat its fruit.

PROVERBS 18:21 (NIV)

Did you know Jesus Christ has already secured our victory over anything that Satan brings at us, especially when it comes to division? He has. When you view your life through that lens, it takes the pressure off and frees you to walk confidently in the strength of the One who has already won. It even changes the way you talk.

If we would all learn to speak words of life, unity, and oneness rather than words of division, fear, and separation, we would experience the victory Christ has already won for us. Rather than speaking in uncertainties, we can now talk with authority and hope. We can, and should, speak words of life.

Words are powerful, after all. Scripture tells us that "death and life are in the power of the tongue" (Proverbs 18:21). Every time you repeat a negative, defeating statement or speak a hopeless thought, you are handing Satan a stick with which to divide you from others and knock you down. Every time you criticize another group, denomination, or race, you are speaking greater dividers into your experience. Every time you disparage a politician, preacher, neighbor, teacher, coworker, or family member, you are erecting walls with your words. We all must learn how to change our thoughts and words if we want to close the gaps that separate us.

Even if you simply say things like, "*If* things get better," or "*If* God comes through," or "I just don't know *if* I'm going to make it," you are giving Satan permission to defeat you. You are giving him permission to defeat us as a collective body of believers in Christ. Rather, God says to use His Word and truth to speak life into our situations. Uncover God's perspective on whatever discord or disunity you are facing and then speak these truths to God, yourself, others, and Satan and his demons.

Speaking something has great significance. Christ said He came to "proclaim release to the captives" (Luke 4:18) shortly before securing it on the cross. Paul instructed us to "proclaim the Lord's death until He comes" (1 Corinthians 11:26) each time we take communion. To proclaim something is to "speak" it, whether through words or actions.

The devil was both defeated and disarmed by Jesus' sacrifice on the cross. He may still have more power than you and I do in our humanity, but the key to understanding spiritual victory in any arena—be it disunity, divide, or opposition—is to recognize that the devil's power means nothing when you understand authority. When Jesus went to the cross, the devil lost his authority. Jesus "disarmed the rulers and authorities" (Colossians 2:15). Not only that, but Colossians 2:15 also tells us that Jesus put them on "display." He held a victory parade. Satan and his demons were put on public exhibition in the spiritual realm as having been defeated.

When we operate out of our victorious, unified position in Christ in the spiritual realm, we are to look at Satan the same way that Jesus sees him. We are to look at him as the loser that he truly is, displayed for all to see.

Put On the Belt of Truth

Lord, let me and all of us who are seeking to bring You honor through a passionate pursuit of unity walk in the authority which Christ secured. It is written in Colossians 2:13-15, "When you were dead in your transgressions and the uncircumcision of your flesh, He made you alive together with Him, having forgiven us all our transgressions, having canceled out the certificate of debt consisting of decrees against us, which was hostile to us; and He has taken it out of the way, having nailed it to the cross. When He had disarmed the rulers and authorities, He made a public display of them, having triumphed over them through Him." We already have the victory over the enemy. Disunity is only due to our lack of faith in the victory Christ has secured. Increase our awareness of the truth of Your Word and increase our faith. In Christ's name and by His authority, I pray this.

Put On the Breastplate of Righteousness

Lord, forgive me when I speak words of doubt, division, and discord. Forgive me for speaking judgment upon others—and even upon myself. Our unity is rooted in the perfect righteousness of Jesus Christ. It is not rooted in humanity's perfection, because there is none. Our righteousness comes from You. Our authority to tap into the benefits of that righteousness comes from You. I ask for You to do what Your Word says in Psalm 141:3: "Set a guard over my mouth, LORD; keep watch over the door of my lips" (NIV). I trust You to align my words, and those of other members of the body of Christ, in Your truth, based on this Scripture. In Christ's name and by His authority, I pray this.

Put On the Shoes of Peace

Lord, "gracious words are a honeycomb, sweet to the soul and healing to the bones" as Proverbs 16:24 (NIV) says. When I speak words of peace, I lay out a pathway for others to walk in that peace. Give me the wisdom I need to change the direction of a conversation when it's heading toward division. Free me from the need to defend myself. Let me remember that peace is preeminent in providing an opportunity for unity to take root. In Christ's name and by His authority, I pray this.

Take Up the Shield of Faith

Lord, a lot of negative self-talk and conversations come about due to fear. When we're afraid, we lash out with our words either to defend or to attack. This then stokes the flames of disunity and division. I ask that You strengthen each of us so we can lift the shield of faith when fear comes calling. Let us know that we are truly loved and secure in You. Let us rest in this truth so we do not turn to words of destruction. I pray not only for myself but for everyone I know. I also pray that you give each of us the faith and wisdom we need to only post words on social media that promote peace and unity. Help us not give in to the temptation to blame, target, troll, put down, or divide through our posts. In Christ's name and by His authority, I pray this.

Take Up the Helmet of Salvation

Father, Revelation 12:10-11 emphasizes the totality and sufficiency of Christ and the salvation He secured for us on the cross when it says, "I heard a loud voice in heaven, saying, 'Now the salvation, and the power, and the kingdom of our God and the authority of His Christ have come, for the accuser of our brethren has been thrown down, he who accuses them before our God day and night. And they overcame him because of the blood of the Lamb and because of the word of their testimony, and they did not love their life even when faced with death.'" Satan and his demons have made it their mission to produce division 24 hours a day, 7 days a week. But this passage reminds us how we are to respond while armed in the full armor of God. We wrestle not against circumstances, people, political issues, or divisions, but against principalities, powers, and forces in the heavenly realm, as Ephesians 6:12 reminds us. In order to overcome anything in our physical world, we need to first overcome Satan because he is the one who is causing the division we face. Help us live in the overcoming power of the Lord Jesus Christ by directing our thoughts and strategies toward the true enemy. In Christ's name and by His authority, I pray this.

Take Up the Sword of the Spirit

Lord, thank You for the sword of the Spirit. Thank You that I can slay every division with the truth of Your Word and the authority of our Savior. I ask that You raise up an army of Bible-literate, truth-believing followers of Jesus Christ who will pray consistently in the Spirit with all power given to us by Jesus Himself. Draw us together across dividing lines so we can reflect to the world what true unity looks like. In Christ's name and by His authority, I pray this.

9

EXTENDING EMPATHY

Blessed be the God and Father of our Lord Jesus Christ,
the Father of mercies and God of all comfort, who
comforts us in all our affliction so that we will be able to
comfort those who are in any affliction with the comfort
with which we ourselves are comforted by God.

2 Corinthians 1:3-4

One of the ways that we overcome our divisions and increase our unity is through the powerful emotional tool of empathy. Empathy defined is the "ability to understand and share the feelings of another."[1] This differs from sympathy, which is defined as "feelings of pity and sorrow for someone else's misfortune."[2] Empathy is a much more comforting approach in relating to another person's situation. The next time you are in a situation where you feel divided from someone else, seek to gain a more compassionate understanding of where they are.

You have probably heard the phrase, "Don't judge someone until you've walked a mile in his shoes." This phrase resonates because each of us is on our own journey of growth. Our perspectives have been shaped by a variety of influences. Our decisions are affected by these perspectives. Thus, you cannot accurately say what you would do in someone else's position because you are not in their position. You have not experienced the hurt, pain, loss, temptations, or trauma that he or she has. Empathy reminds us of our humanity and helps us allow space for another's place in life. When you see someone who is projecting anger, division, or blame, make a mental note to guide yourself toward a more empathic response, acknowledging the source of hurt within them.

In John 11, we see Mary weeping because her brother Lazarus had died. She was weeping for a couple of reasons. One was because she had lost her dearly loved brother. But another reason was that her dear friend, Jesus, could have saved him but didn't come to help when He had been called to do so. I'm sure Mary's emotions were a mixture of sadness and feelings of betrayal and loss. In fact, Mary was so hurt that when she finally did see Jesus, she cast blame on Him and told Him that if He had been there, her brother would not have died (verse 32).

Jesus' response to Mary's accusation gives us great insight into the importance of authentic empathy in the face of divisive words or actions. We read, "When Jesus therefore saw her weeping, and the Jews who came with her also weeping, He was deeply moved in spirit and was troubled, and said, 'Where have you laid him?' They said to Him, 'Lord, come and see.' Jesus wept" (verses 33-35).

Jesus didn't offer Mary a sermon on the importance of letting go. He didn't scold her for the mixed bag of her emotions spilling over into words of blame and anger. When Jesus saw the pain in those around Him, He became moved in His spirit and troubled to the point of weeping Himself.

Why did God weep? After all, wouldn't Christ, the God-man, know that death is just a passageway into eternity? Couldn't He, of all people, have sat back and nonchalantly said, "Hey, it's going to be okay"? But Jesus wept even though He knew all this and more because He saw their pain. He empathized with their hurt. He felt their loss on this side of eternity.

As you seek to be a unifying bridge to those whose paths are littered with pain and loss, you must first offer empathy from a place of authentic care. You do this by recognizing that the pain in those around you is real, even if you know it may not be rational. Pain is pain, and other people's feelings need an empathic response. The worst thing you can do for someone in a place of pain, anger, blame, or divisiveness is tell them that their position is not justified. Instead, become like Jesus who—knowing the end from the beginning and knowing that Lazarus would live again—wept with those who wept. And in His weeping, He brought empathy at the time it was needed most.

Put On the Belt of Truth

> Lord, I know Your Word tells us that we are to empathize with others. Romans 12:15 states this truth as an instruction on how we are to live: "Rejoice with those who rejoice, and weep with those who weep." Empathy combines many of Your attributes and many of the qualities You call us to live out as Your kingdom disciples. First Peter 3:8-9 lists some of them: "To sum up, all of you be harmonious, sympathetic, brotherly, kindhearted, and humble in spirit; not returning evil for evil or insult for insult, but giving a blessing instead; for you were called for the very purpose that you might inherit a blessing." When our hearts reflect a true understanding of who we are in Christ, we can give a blessing when we are wronged, knowing that You allow everything to transpire. I pray for my heart, and the hearts of all those in Your collective body, to reflect these attributes. In Christ's name and by His authority, I pray this.

Put On the Breastplate of Righteousness

> Father, Jesus came to fulfill the law, not to abolish it, as
> Matthew 5:17 reminds us. He came that He might give
> us a standard of righteousness rooted in Him. He has
> called us to take up this breastplate of righteousness
> in every moment of our lives, and that righteousness is
> identified by love for You and others. As a result, we live
> righteously when we offer empathy rather than judgment,
> bringing about unity by taking on another's legitimate
> moral burdens in any way we can. Galatians 6:2 states it
> clearly: "Bear one another's burdens, and thereby fulfill the
> law of Christ." Let this be so in our churches and personal
> lives. In Christ's name and by His authority, I pray this.

Put On the Shoes of Peace

> Lord, I thank You that Jesus modeled for me what I should
> do when someone accuses or blames me. Thank You
> that Jesus did not get defensive when Martha and Mary
> spoke harmful and accusatory words to Him, but rather
> demonstrated how to preserve peace by responding
> in empathy. Thank You that Jesus serves as a model
> of peace-filled living I can follow in order to be an
> instrument of Your peace in all I do and say. Please
> keep me aware of this truth and the need for a peaceful
> response to any blame, division, or hate speech that
> comes my way. Show me how not only to turn the other
> cheek but also to empathize with the emotions of the
> ones bound by so much pain. May I be a vessel used
> by You to free them with Your love and peace. I pray
> Colossians 3:15 for my own life and for the lives of all
> Your followers: "Let the peace of Christ rule in your hearts,

to which indeed you were called in one body; and be thankful." In Christ's name and by His authority, I pray this.

Take Up the Shield of Faith

God, I take up the shield of faith against division, knowing that when I walk according to the precepts in Your Word, I will walk in the full victory of unity as far as it depends upon me. Colossians 3:12-14 speaks of this truth and reminds me that I am to walk by faith. "As those who have been chosen of God, holy and beloved, put on a heart of compassion, kindness, humility, gentleness and patience; bearing with one another, and forgiving each other, whoever has a complaint against anyone; just as the Lord forgave you, so also should you. Beyond all these things put on love, which is the perfect bond of unity." I know this bond of unity is attainable by the authority of Jesus Christ when I live my life under His overarching rule of love. In Christ's name and by His authority, I pray this.

Take Up the Helmet of Salvation

Father, today I put on the helmet of salvation and reject every thought or painful memory that drags me into division, blame, or opposition. I pray that in the security given to me by the blood of Jesus Christ I will freely allow myself to empathize with those who have walked a different journey than mine. Your salvation covers all, and I need to live according to the truth of Your salvation, rather than place greater importance on some people or groups over others. Forgive me for where I have judged and You have not. Forgive me for where I have turned a cold heart and You have wept. Forgive me for

where I have blamed and You have been burdened.
In Christ's name and by His authority, I pray this.

Take Up the Sword of the Spirit

Lord, by the mighty sword of the Spirit I take captive
every divisive attack of the enemy. I speak what is written
in Hebrews 13:3 into my divisions: "Remember those
who are in prison, as though in prison with them, and
those who are mistreated, since you also are in the
body" (ESV). Whether these are prisons of self-doubt,
identity loss, financial struggle, anger, hate, immorality,
elitism, or anything else, I remember each person with
empathy, knowing that we are all one in the body of
Christ. In Christ's name and by His authority, I pray this.

10

RELINQUISHING IDOLS

You shall have no other gods before Me.
You shall not make for yourself an idol, or any
likeness of what is in heaven above or on the earth
beneath or in the water under the earth.

Exodus 20:3-4

I have some bad news: Christians have lost their home-field advantage. In sports, a team wants to play on their home field or court because they will get the maximum support from their hometown fans. They will be cheered and encouraged. The other team will have to try and play amid the roar of their rivals' fans as it drowns out their communication.

Home-field advantage provides a team with the opportunity to move forward toward victory in a unified way. In fact, some football teams have given their fans a number, referring to them as the twelfth player because the fans' cheering, roaring, and yelling help the home team in their strategy to win.

There was a time when Christianity in America had the home-field advantage. The Judeo-Christian ethic and worldview dominated the environment. However, believers have progressively lost that advantage. Christianity is no longer the normative worldview in the country. In fact, kingdom values are constantly resisted and rejected from every direction and on every front.

Christianity is a minority belief system in a predominantly pagan society. Educational institutes, media, and celebrity spokespeople successfully seek to marginalize biblical views. They have done this to such a degree that many Christians use the name but basically spend their time changing uniforms to play for the other team. Many believers and churchgoers chase the American idols of me-ism, humanism, and materialism. They bow before these idols rather than following the example of Shadrach, Meshach, and Abednego, who refused to bow before the golden statue of Nebuchadnezzar (see Daniel 3).

Everyone who reads this book is affected by this cultural shift. Each of us is being influenced by the idols of a society that is anti-God and rejects the truths found in God's Word. So subtle and so pervasive are these idols that many people worship them without even realizing they have knelt.

We worship society's idols anytime we place societal expectations and behavioral norms above God's. We worship them when we allow or even promote division due to disagreements or differing opinions based on preference. We worship them when we do not place unity as one of our chief aims and highest values. We bow to the idols of culture when we kneel before rhetoric meant to split brothers and sisters in Christ.

In order to stand tall and tear down the idols of me-ism and division in our nation, we must return to speaking words of respect, honor, and truth. We must learn to live underneath the comprehensive rule of God over every area of life. We must seek His approval, not man's. We must turn off the noise that is meant to distance us from one another and find instead our common ground as humans made in the image of a triune, loving, and unified God.

Put On the Belt of Truth

Thank You, Lord, for the mercies that come from Your throne. Thank You that we can stand in the truth of 1 John 1:9, that if we confess our sins, You are righteous and just to forgive us our sins and cleanse us from all unrighteousness. We have become a nation and church body given to idolatry. Our idols come in many forms. Satan has used them to divide our allegiance, removing our attention from You and raising up divisions between us. Psalm 135:15-18 states the truth about these idols (whether ideas, race, beliefs, groups, or possessions) and those who have set them up: "The idols of the nations are but silver and gold, the work of man's hands. They have mouths, but they do not speak; they have eyes, but they do not see; they have ears, but they do not hear, nor is there any breath at all in their mouths. Those who make them will be like them, yes, everyone who trusts in them." Our idols do not have the authority others claim they have. You have that authority, Jesus, and in Your name I ask that the idols in our culture and in my own heart be taken down and demolished. In Christ's name and by His authority, I pray this.

Put On the Breastplate of Righteousness

Lord, I put on the breastplate of righteousness, which serves as a weapon of discernment. Idols of division do not only come about through our thoughts, beliefs, or systems—they also come about through people. I pray for a spirit of righteous discernment to be unleashed upon Your followers. As it is written in 1 John 4:1, "Beloved, do not believe every spirit, but test the spirits to see whether they are from God, because many false prophets have gone out into the world." Open my eyes to see and recognize the false prophets around me and the false messages being spread in Your name. Help us all discern true righteousness, because it is in true righteousness that unity will thrive. In Christ's name and by His authority, I pray this.

Put On the Shoes of Peace

Thank You, God, that peace is a gift we all can enjoy and experience when we turn our hearts, minds, and eyes away from idols and focus them instead on You. Give me the boldness to walk in peace by not acquiescing to my culture's idols. Give our churches the boldness to stand for peace by not promoting idolatry. Reveal to our nation and the world the abundance of Your peace by keeping our hearts pure, refining us in Your power, and tearing down the idols erected against Your truth and righteousness. In Christ's name and by His authority, I pray this.

Take Up the Shield of Faith

Father God, I take up the shield of faith against the idols in my own life and those in my surrounding culture. This faith is rooted in the truth of Your Word, which boldly declares an idol's lack of authority, the demise of those who raise up idols or follow them, and the ultimate authority of Christ over all. Isaiah 44:9-11 states, "Those who fashion a graven image are all of them futile, and their precious things are of no profit; even their own witnesses fail to see or know, so that they will be put to shame. Who has fashioned a god or cast an idol to no profit? Behold, all his companions will be put to shame, for the craftsmen themselves are mere men. Let them all assemble themselves, let them stand up, let them tremble, let them together be put to shame." In faith, I turn from idols and trust that Your swift judgment is being carried out on all who have lifted up idols to divide us in the body of Christ and in our nation and world. In Christ's name and by His authority, I pray this.

Take Up the Helmet of Salvation

Lord, I ask You to guard my mind from falling for idols of division through the power of the helmet of Your salvation. Christ has secured on the cross enough authority for me to rebuke the idols of division that creep into my thoughts. I embrace love. I embrace unity. I embrace forgiveness. I embrace humility. Let all of these and the attributes of Your Spirit guide and guard my mind in You. In Christ's name and by His authority, I pray this.

Take Up the Sword of the Spirit

Heavenly Father, I take up the sword of the Spirit in my battle to tear down idols that promote division, judgment, blame, and resentment. I refute the idols of false doctrine and stand in the gap for those who need to be freed, as it is written in Colossians 2:8, "See to it that no one takes you captive through philosophy and empty deception, according to the tradition of men, according to the elementary principles of the world, rather than according to Christ." May I and all those who are called to be kingdom disciples set an example of purity for others to follow, as it is written in Acts 15:29, "Abstain from things sacrificed to idols and from blood and from things strangled and from fornication; if you keep yourselves free from such things, you will do well." In Christ's name and by His authority, I pray this.

11

LETTING GO OF OFFENSES

Bear with each other and forgive one another if any of you has a grievance against someone. Forgive as the Lord forgave you.

COLOSSIANS 3:13 (NIV)

A tremendous amount of division comes from bitterness. When someone offends (sins against) us, it often breeds bitterness, which, in turn, erects walls of separation. These sins can be personal or corporate or even generational. Thus, letting go of past offenses is similar to draining the pus out of a wound. It allows the wound to heal because it denies the further growth of harmful bacteria.

We call this choice to let go "forgiveness." Biblical forgiveness is the decision to no longer credit an offense against an offender with a view of enacting vengeance. It also involves releasing that person from a debt owed as well as the blame they deserve due to an infraction or sin committed against you. Keep in mind, forgiveness is a decision. It is not first and foremost an emotion. It's not about how you are feeling at any given moment but rather about the choice you have made to no longer credit an offense against an offender—even if that offender is yourself.

The most accurate definition of forgiveness is found in

1 Corinthians 13, where we read about love. In verse 5 we see that love "keeps no record of wrongs" (NIV). That is not to say that love justifies the wrong committed. No, that's called *enablement*. Love never justifies wrong or says it's okay. That would ignore the standard of righteousness God calls His followers to live out and undermine your own personal worth by denying you were wronged. Love also doesn't skip over sin and pretend it didn't happen. Like an alcoholic's spouse continuing to clean up the mess from each previous disaster, this only provides the opportunity for the offense to continue. And that's not love either.

Letting go means you do not keep a record of the sin. You do not record it, revisit it, rehash it, or get revenge because of it. God forgives us in this way. He strikes the offense from our account, letting go of it. That is not to say He forgets it happened. But we are not indebted to pay Him for it. Jesus paid the penalty and price of it in our place.

Now, letting go of an offense against you (or an offense against a group to which you belong) takes on different forms depending on the situation. It doesn't always mean you will relate to the person the same way you did before the offense. But it does mean you no longer hold the offense against them—whether in your heart through your emotions or in an attitude of anger, revenge, guilt, or shame. Instead, you choose to love them.

By letting go of the offense against you, you are free to demonstrate love through how you speak of the offender and how you take them before the Lord in prayer. Whatever the offense, remaining in the midst of the mess through unforgiveness will only widen the divide between you. It's time to forgive.

Put On the Belt of Truth

Thank You, Lord, for not hiding the truth we need in order to live as victorious kingdom disciples of Yours. One of the ways we overcome the divisions between us is by following Your Word and applying it in our lives. Luke 6:27 says clearly, "Love your enemies, do good to those who hate you." We cannot love our enemies and do good to those who hate us if we refuse to let go of the offenses done against us. I want to walk in Your truth and wear this piece of spiritual armor every moment of my life, so I choose now to let go of the offenses done against me by the authority of Christ. I choose to embrace the rule of love You have called me to obey. Will you open up an opportunity for me to "do good" to those who have committed an offense against me in the past? I would like to pass all the tests of love You send my way, knowing that each time I do it will make it easier and easier to continue to walk in unity with everyone I know. In Christ's name and by His authority, I pray this.

Put On the Breastplate of Righteousness

Lord, it's easy to look around at other people and see what they have done wrong. It's easy to judge and hold offenses against people. But there is only one Judge, and that is You, as James 4:12 reminds me. When I choose not to release others of their offenses, I am promoting disunity because I am raising myself higher than Your preeminent position. Let me remember what true righteousness looks like by focusing on how You view offenses and those who commit them. Psalm 103:8-12 describes how You let go of offenses when it says, "The LORD is compassionate and gracious, slow to anger and abounding in lovingkindness. He will not always strive with us, nor will He keep His anger forever. He has not dealt with us according to our sins, nor rewarded us according to our iniquities. For as high as the heavens are above the earth, so great is His lovingkindness toward those who fear Him. As far as the east is from the west, so far has He removed our transgressions from us." May I, and all those who are called by Your name, live according to the precepts in this passage and Your forgiving, compassionate love. In Christ's name and by His authority, I pray this.

Put On the Shoes of Peace

Thank You, Lord, that I can walk in peace when I embrace the truth of Your compassion and forgiveness. Thank You that I do not need to live with bitterness in my soul. I can let it go. I can release the hurt and pain caused by offenses against me or others. When I do, I am assured of the peace that will fill my soul and mark my pathways with calm and unity. Alert me to every step I take in the direction of division and resentment so I will be convicted and turn toward Your love. Reveal to me the abundance of Your compassion so it will overflow to others as well. Remind me of the countless times You have forgiven me and let go of the offenses I have committed against You and others as well. This reminder will help me live with a heart of gratitude, giving me what I need in order to walk according to the model You set before me. In Christ's name and by His authority, I pray this.

Take Up the Shield of Faith

Father God, Jesus taught us the connection between the forgiveness we've received and the forgiveness we need to show others. We read about this in Matthew 6:12,14, which says, "'Forgive us our debts, as we also have forgiven our debtors'...For if you forgive others for their transgressions, your heavenly Father will also forgive you." This is the shield of faith I must take up when I choose to forgive others, knowing that if I let go of the offenses of others, You also are doing the same for me. I know there are times when the offenses done against me or others will need to be addressed by You. I take up the shield of faith in these instances, as well, by choosing to let go of those offenses, because You say in Romans 12:19, "Never take your own revenge, beloved, but leave room for the wrath of God, for it is written, 'Vengeance is Mine, I will repay,' says the Lord." The shield of faith leaves room for You to correct, discipline, and restore as needed. I choose to let go and give You space to address the offenses at hand. In Christ's name and by His authority, I pray this.

Take Up the Helmet of Salvation

Lord, I am secure through Jesus Christ, who gave Himself as a sacrifice for me. On the cross, He chose to die for the sins of humanity. He chose not to hold our offenses against us, but rather to let them go by paying for them on our behalf. Thank You for Jesus and the assurance of forgiveness I have through Him. Let me look to this helmet of salvation as a reminder that I have no right to hold someone else's offenses against them. Jesus died for those offenses and sins just as He died for mine. In Christ's name and by His authority, I pray this.

Take Up the Sword of the Spirit

Heavenly Father, I pick up the sword of the Spirit and boldly declare that the enemy does not have authority to promote gossip and slander in the body of Christ. Your Word says in Proverbs 17:9, "He who conceals a transgression seeks love, but he who repeats a matter separates intimate friends." When we openly speak of offenses and sins in order to discredit others, we breed greater division and fear among ourselves. Let the sword of Your Word penetrate deep into my heart. Help me speak words of life and redirect conversations that come up in my presence or on social media toward that which promotes unity through a shared heart of humility, forgiveness, and grace. In Christ's name and by His authority, I pray this.

12

A CLEAN HEART

Create in me a clean heart, O God,
and renew a steadfast spirit within me.

Psalm 51:10

Perhaps you struggle with allergies. I certainly do. Allergies occur when dust or pollen in the atmosphere creates misery within the body. Stuffy nose, runny eyes, and congested airways present themselves for reckoning all because the air has been contaminated with something the body cannot process well.

Many of us wrestle with allergies simply because this world is not pure. But worse than physical allergies are spiritual allergies. These take root in our souls when our hearts are not pure. The word *pure* refers to something that is free from defect. When contamination runs amok in our spiritual systems, it leads to watery spiritual eyes and an inability to see God for who He really is.

Jesus spoke about it this way: "Blessed are the pure in heart, for they shall see God" (Matthew 5:8). In this powerful statement, He taught us that only those who live with an undivided and undefiled heart and with a singleness of devotion to the Lord will see God.

Jesus didn't say that those without sin will see God. Rather, He said that those who are pure in heart will see Him. We all sin. But sin and God are irreconcilable. The two don't get along.

It's sort of like the garbage in your house. I hope you don't get along with it for too long, or your house is going to smell. I would imagine you take the garbage out once or twice a week like I do, removing it so that your house does not become a trash dump. Similarly, sin is a reality we all deal with. We were born in sin and have a sin nature. But when sin does show up in your life, I hope you don't hang out with it. Like trash, it is wise to address it and remove it from your life through prayer and repentance, turning from it.

Being pure means not allowing defects to penetrate the heart, which would cause God to distance Himself from intimacy with us. Far too many believers carry on a long-distance relationship with God. The distance exists due to a lack of purity in the heart. When personal sin is allowed to linger, rot, mold, and grow, it brings damage to everything near it. Much of the division we find in our homes, churches, and culture today has its root in sin. We're too busy pointing fingers at everyone else, failing to realize that our personal sin distances God's relational presence and power from us.

Without God's relational presence and power, we cannot obtain the high callings of unity, forgiveness, and preserving the peace—because the spirit may be willing, but the flesh is weak (Matthew 26:41). We must humbly depend upon God to work through us if we are to live as vessels of peace and unity in our homes, our workplaces, and our nation. Yet that starts with a clean heart, pure before the Lord and in an ongoing pursuit of personal holiness.

Unity starts with you. It starts with me. It starts with each of us getting right with God, living under His rule, abiding in Him, and allowing His Spirit to dominate all we think, say, and do.

One way we overcome disunity is by authentically returning to God for the forgiveness of our sins and living with a clean heart.

Focusing on outward religious ritual will only lead to a greater opportunity for division. Cleaning must take place on the inside first, and then it will overflow to the outward actions—which will lead to real change, healing, and unity.

Put On the Belt of Truth

Today, Lord, I pray for all of us who need to have our hearts cleansed by You. I pray against the falsehoods of selfishness and narcissism that plague our culture and social media platforms. Deliver us from self-absorption and create in us a clean heart and willing spirit to do Your will—which is to promote unity. You desire that we live as one. I ask that the truth of Your Word be made manifest today in my own life and the collective church body and our nation, according to Ezekiel 36:25-27, which states, "I will sprinkle clean water on you, and you will be clean; I will cleanse you from all your impurities and from all your idols. I will give you a new heart and put a new spirit in you; I will remove from you your heart of stone and give you a heart of flesh. And I will put my Spirit in you and move you to follow my decrees and be careful to keep my laws" (NIV). May Your truth define us and come to pass in our lives. In Christ's name and by His authority, I pray this.

Put On the Breastplate of Righteousness

Lord, may our hearts be righteous. May my heart be clean before You. Show me where I need to address sin in my own heart. Convict me so I will be brought to repentance before You. I do not want to be like the Pharisees whom You condemned. Matthew 23:27 reveals how You feel about an unclean heart: "Woe to you, teachers of the law and Pharisees, you hypocrites! You are like whitewashed tombs, which look beautiful on the outside but on the inside are full of the bones of the dead and everything unclean" (NIV). Righteousness starts in the heart. Defend my heart from the attacks of the enemy as he seeks to create bitterness, jealousy, envy, pride, division, and blame. Restore to me a clean heart so I can carry the breastplate of righteousness wherever I go, thus promoting unity in all I do. In Christ's name and by His authority, I pray this.

Put On the Shoes of Peace

Today, Lord, I put on the shoes of peace for myself and my relationships and all with whom I come into contact. I choose to wear shoes of peace rooted in a clean heart, revealing the fruit of the Spirit to all around me. The fruit of the Spirit cannot grow in an environment that is dirty with sin. That's why I seek You to clean my heart so I can produce this good fruit listed in Galatians 5:22-23: "The fruit of the Spirit is love, joy, peace, patience, kindness, goodness, faithfulness, gentleness, self-control." Make us all live in such a way that we bear much fruit in Your body. In Christ's name and by His authority, I pray this.

Take Up the Shield of Faith

Father, You see the many missiles the enemy fires at us to stir up dissension, create division, and separate us from one another in the home, workplace, church, community, nation, and world. I take up the shield of faith, knowing that unity starts with me. Rather than focusing on fixing other people, Lord, I choose to be personally responsible for my contribution to our unity efforts. I know if I focus on my own ability to live in faith with a clean heart under

Your overarching kingdom rule, I will be contributing to the unity we all seek. Help me not get distracted and point out other people who have fallen away, as if I am the only one seeking to be clean. No, I have faith that there are many others seeking unity like me and, together, we will achieve it when we begin by cleaning our own lives and hearts. In Christ's name and by His authority, I pray this.

Take Up the Helmet of Salvation

Lord, I put on the helmet of salvation to protect my mind and heart from anything that could pull me away from Your call to live purely and righteously, which is possible because of the blood of the Lamb. When shame or guilt mocks my attempts to live with a clean heart, remind me to take up the helmet of salvation, knowing that Jesus' sacrifice covers all my sin. I can be cleansed entirely of anything and everything I have ever done wrong because Christ's blood covers all. Help others know this truth and be protected by it too. In Christ's name and by His authority, I pray this.

Take Up the Sword of the Spirit

Lord, the attacks on unity in all areas are severe. I raise the sword of the Spirit against the enemy, for it is written in Matthew 5:8, "Blessed are the pure in heart, for they shall see God." I know that when we see Your hand and what You are doing to unite us across all enemy-inspired divides between us, we will offer You praise. You have told us how important it is to have a clean heart in this fight, for it is written in Proverbs 4:23, "Watch over your heart with all diligence, for from it flow the springs of life." May we all watch over our hearts, guarding them from deception and destruction so the springs of life and unity may flow freely among us as a people under You. In Christ's name and by His authority, I pray this.

13

FORGIVING THOSE WHO HAVE HURT YOU

God was in Christ reconciling the world to Himself, not counting their trespasses against them, and He has committed to us the word of reconciliation.

2 Corinthians 5:19

When someone has hurt you, you can offer one of two types of forgiveness: unilateral forgiveness or transactional forgiveness. Unilateral forgiveness involves forgiving someone who has not requested your forgiveness and may not have even repented of their offense. You are granting them forgiveness on your own—unilaterally, or without their involvement.

Why would you grant forgiveness to someone who hasn't asked for it and probably doesn't deserve it? Here's the main reason: You do it not to set them free but to set yourself free. Internal wholeness is key to achieving external unity and oneness with others. Thus, you grant unilateral forgiveness so you can keep going. This releases you from something the other person may never get right. This is what God did on the cross by "not counting their trespasses against them" (2 Corinthians 5:19).

There are other reasons for offering forgiveness unilaterally. The offense might be so small that it's not worth addressing with the other person. Or maybe the offender has died or can't be contacted. Or perhaps the offender simply won't repent, apologize, or even acknowledge what they have done.

In situations like these, if you are unable to unilaterally forgive, you are the one who is held hostage, not the offender. It has been said that resentment is like drinking poison and expecting someone else to die from it. But of course, you are only poisoning yourself. The bitterness, regret, and anger churning inside you poison your thoughts, override your emotions, distract you from living a life of unity, and create divisions in your relationships with others.

You cannot change what happened to you, nor can you change the person who did it. You can only change yourself and your response to the offense, so that is where you need to focus. Unilateral forgiveness doesn't just release the other person—unilateral forgiveness releases you.

The second type of forgiveness is transactional forgiveness, which can be given when the offender has repented and sought out your forgiveness. In other words, a transaction is taking place. It is a two-way agreement.

Transactional forgiveness restores something that has been broken. People who willingly confess and repent *usually* want the relationship to be reconciled. But here's the trick—we don't always know the real motive behind the offender's confession and repentance. The motivation may be pure, and the person could be truly repentant. Then again, perhaps the offender simply got caught and is trying to avoid the consequences.

That's why it's important to test the fruit of repentance before entering into reconciliation. This is what Joseph did when his brothers asked him to forgive them in Egypt. In Genesis 42:15-16, Joseph said he was testing their words—finding out whether they were telling the truth. At that time, his brothers weren't aware he was the brother they had lied about and sold into slavery. But Joseph knew who they were and what they had done to him 22 years earlier. Because of that, he tested their hearts and character to see whether they had changed or remained the same.

Saying "I'm sorry for what I did" is a good thing. But if that apology is not accompanied by fruits of repentance, it might really mean "I'm sorry I got caught."

True repentance leads to life. For example, after Peter denied Jesus three times, he went out and wept—and then he returned to serving Christ. On the other hand, Judas merely felt remorse (Matthew 27:3)—and then he went out and hanged himself.

Before you restore a relationship with someone who seeks transactional forgiveness from you, take time to make sure they are offering true repentance and not just remorse. It is important to see whether they have truly turned from the sin they committed against you so the cycle of division is no longer perpetuated.

Put On the Belt of Truth

> I praise You, Lord, that You do not hold my sins
> against me. You do not stand in judgment against me,
> condemning me as I deserve. Rather, Your forgiveness
> frees me to fully live out the life You have designed for me
> to enjoy. You have set me free through the sacrifice of
> Jesus Christ, so help me not hold others in bondage, as
> Matthew 18:23-35 reminds me. The truth of Your Word
> makes it clear how You feel about unforgiveness in my
> heart when it says in verse 35, "My heavenly Father will
> also do the same to you, if each of you does not forgive
> his brother from your heart." I do not want to live as a

hypocrite who receives forgiveness but refuses to give it, contributing to the divisions among us rather than seeking unity. In Christ's name and by His authority, I pray this.

Put On the Breastplate of Righteousness

God, I trust in the breastplate of righteousness You provide as I live in freedom from bitterness, envy, strife, and judgment. Make me a vessel for unity in our world. Make me a light that shines in the darkness of division. Your Word states the importance of forgiveness when it says in Matthew 18:21-22, "Peter came and said to Him, 'Lord, how often shall my brother sin against me and I forgive him? Up to seven times?' Jesus said to him, 'I do not say to you, up to seven times, but up to seventy times seven.'" Forgiveness is not a one-time event. Help me be mindful that righteousness involves an ongoing renewing of my heart in the spirit of forgiveness. In this way, I will help unify the body of Christ through the power of oneness. In Christ's name and by His authority, I pray this.

Put On the Shoes of Peace

I praise You, Lord, for the opportunity to wear the shoes of peace. Make me aware of the presence of peace in my surroundings so I can affirm and validate it. Help me contribute to that peace through what I say and do. Make my thoughts be ones of peace toward all others. I pray that others will have thoughts of peace toward me. When divisive speech arises, help me direct the situation toward peace. Allow my life to reflect Your peace always. In Christ's name and by His authority, I pray this.

Take Up the Shield of Faith

God, I rejoice in how the shield of faith stops every divisive arrow the enemy throws at me. I know You are strong enough to deflect any attack the enemy makes to cause division in my relationships and in the corporate body of Christ. By faith I believe that my sins are so far removed through Your forgiveness that they do not create new negative consequences for me, because it is written in Psalm 103:12, "As far as the east is from the west, so far has He removed our transgressions from us." Let me show this same grace to those who have sinned against me either personally or through systems of injustice. In Christ's name and by His authority, I pray this.

Take Up the Helmet of Salvation

Lord, Satan wants to create division in the body of Christ by increasing our insecurities, jealousy, disagreements, and sense of competition. Rather than letting go and resting in the security that comes through identification with Jesus, we let the enemy promote doubt, fear, and envy among us. I resist and rebuke the enemy's attacks in the name of Jesus. I am secure in Christ, and I am loved. Let everyone else who is in Christ also be assured of their full acceptance in You so they can then be used by You as an instrument of unity and love. In Christ's name and by His authority, I pray this.

Take Up the Sword of the Spirit

Father, with every attack Satan launches to promote division, I take up Your Word, which is the sword of the Spirit. With that sword, my victory in spiritual warfare is guaranteed. Sharpen my sword, Lord. Keep me diligent to wield it at the first sign of attack on our unity. I use Your Word this very minute against Satan, quoting Colossians 1:13-14, which says, "He rescued us from the domain of darkness, and transferred us to the kingdom of His beloved Son, in whom we have redemption, the forgiveness of sins." In Christ's name and by His authority, I pray this.

14

INCREASING CONNECTION

*God has so composed the body, giving more abundant honor to
that member which lacked, so that there may be no division in the
body, but that the members may have the same care for one another.*

1 CORINTHIANS 12:24-25

We're living in a day when connection has become a pretty big deal. Now, I'm not computer savvy but I do know enough to know that the Internet and smartphones have made connecting a priority of everyday life. Computers and tablets and smartphones, Instagram and Pinterest and Twitter…digital media have dominated our connectivity and raised it to another level. All day long, people are communicating with each other through texts, chats, e-mails, and more. People you know will tag you, and people you don't know hashtag things that interest you. As this happens, your desire for connectivity continues to grow. This is because each of us innately hungers for this connection.

We recognize the desire for relationship in our connectivity-crazy culture, but this hunger is not new to twenty-first-century social media. It started with something God had in mind when He created us. This is explained for us in detail in 1 Corinthians 12, which is the most comprehensive statement in the New Testament on the importance of connecting with others in a spirit of unity. This subject is so critical to overcoming divisions that the Holy Spirit directed the apostle Paul to commit the entire chapter to the priority of connectivity. The visual image of it can be summarized in verse 27: "Now you are Christ's body, and individually members of it."

When God sets out to give us an illustration of connectivity, He uses something all of us can identify with—a body. Each of us has a physical body, so each of us knows that the body does what the head tells it to do. If the head says, "Walk," the body walks. If the head says, "Raise your arm," the body raises its arm. In other words, our bodies are completely responsive to our brains.

When your brain says one thing and your body does something else, you need to see a doctor. The job of the physical body is to reflect the dictates of the brain. A body divided against itself will not be able to carry out the most basic functions, let alone enjoy the life God has provided. The same is true with the collective body of Christ. When we live in a divided state of being, we prevent ourselves from having a positive impact on society. We limit our expressions of love. We cannot blame anyone but ourselves for our ineffectiveness because a body is only as strong as it is united—each member honoring and cherishing the others.

Scripture is clear that Jesus Christ is the head of the church, which He calls His body. Therefore, the job of Jesus' body—that's us—is to reflect the dictates of our head, Jesus Christ. To do anything else is dysfunction. To do anything else produces chaos, confusion, and pain. Only when we are properly aligned underneath the goals, visions, and directives of Jesus Christ do we fully function as we were designed. Yet this can only be done in a spirit of connectivity. We must unite as one under the headship of Jesus Christ.

Put On the Belt of Truth

The truth is, Lord, that You have called us to unity. You have created us for oneness. We are to live with one mind, connected to one another, focused on Your love and the greater good of all. Your Word states this clearly in 1 Corinthians 1:10, where it says, "Now I exhort you, brethren, by the name of our Lord Jesus Christ, that you all agree and that there be no divisions among you, but that you be made complete in the same mind and in the same judgment." I ask that You help all of us who are called by Your name to live without divisions among us. Help us "be made complete in the same mind and in the same judgment," rooted in Your Word and Your truth. Let falsehood and lies be obvious to all. Give us discernment to know truth, which originates from You. In Christ's name and by His authority, I pray this.

Put On the Breastplate of Righteousness

Lord, You tell me in Your Word that Your blood purifies us of all sin and opens the door for connection and unity. First John 1:7 describes it this way: "If we walk in the Light as He Himself is in the Light, we have fellowship with one another, and the blood of Jesus His Son cleanses us from all sin." Our fellowship is to be rooted in Your light and righteousness. Lord Jesus, shine Your light in our hearts. Drive out the darkness of division. Let the righteousness that comes from Your light thoroughly eradicate divisiveness, isolation, pride, and rebellion from my heart and from the hearts of all those who are called by Your name and cleansed by Your blood. In Christ's name and by His authority, I pray this.

Put On the Shoes of Peace

Thank You, God, that when I walk in peace, unity is the outcome. I do not need to force unity. The Spirit Himself has created it. All I need to do is walk in peace, and the unity You have created will be preserved. Let peace be my guide in all I think, say, and do. Romans 12:16 clearly states Your will: "Be of the same mind toward one another; do not be haughty in mind, but associate with the lowly. Do not be wise in your own estimation." Make this verse a reality for myself and all those who follow You. In Christ's name and by His authority, I pray this.

Take Up the Shield of Faith

Father God, when we connect with other believers and together hold up the shield of faith, we become even stronger as we seek to break down the walls that divide us. Paul wrote of this sharing of faith in Romans 1:11-12, which says, "I long to see you so that I may impart some spiritual gift to you, that you may be established; that is, that I may be encouraged together with you while among you, each of us by the other's faith, both yours and mine." May we in the body of Christ be encouraged together and lift up the shield of faith so we are more unified than ever before and are able to defeat the destructive forces that seek to divide us. In Christ's name and by His authority, I pray this.

Take Up the Helmet of Salvation

Lord, my salvation started with the unity found in the Trinity. Because Jesus willingly surrendered to Your will and sacrificed Himself on the cross, and because You honored that sacrifice, I am able to take up the helmet of salvation. Help me not dishonor the sacrifice of salvation by living a life punctuated by disunity. Let me model the unity set forth by You so others may also come to know You and the power of Your salvation in their own lives. In Christ's name and by His authority, I pray this.

Take Up the Sword of the Spirit

Heavenly Father, I take up the sword of the Spirit against Satan and quote Hebrews 10:24-25, which says, "Let us consider how to stimulate one another to love and good deeds, not forsaking our own assembling together, as is the habit of some, but encouraging one another; and all the more as you see the day drawing near." I raise this sword by intentionally seeking community and connectivity with others in the body of Christ. It is also written in 1 Peter 4:7-9, "The end of all things is near; therefore, be of sound judgment and sober spirit for the purpose of prayer. Above all, keep fervent in your love for one another, because love covers a multitude of sins. Be hospitable to one another without complaint." Make me a person of sober spirit, engaging in prayer, loving others fully, and being hospitable to everyone. In Christ's name and by His authority, I pray this.

15

THE BLESSINGS OF ONENESS

Behold, how good and how pleasant it is
for brothers to dwell together in unity!

PSALM 133:1

Oneness brings with it many blessings. One is power. In fact, we see that even God recognizes how powerful oneness is when we read in Genesis 11 about the time when all the people on the earth used the same language. They gathered together and decided to build a city with a tower that would reach into heaven.

God's response to what they were doing is recorded for us. He said, "Behold, they are one people, and they all have the same language. And this is what they began to do, and now nothing which they purpose to do will be impossible for them" (verse 6). God then confused their language and scattered them over the whole earth because He knew that oneness is powerful. Nothing expresses the principle of the power of oneness as much as this incident at Babel, because if God recognizes its power and importance in history when embraced among unbelievers operating in rebellion against Him, then how much more important and powerful is it for us?

Another blessing of living in unity is letting the world know about the King under whom we serve. Oneness brings glory to God by moving us into the atmosphere where we can experience God's response in such a way that He manifests His glory most fully in history. All the praying, preaching, worship, or Bible studies in the world can never bring about the fullest possible manifestation of God's presence like functioning in a spirit of oneness in the body of Christ. This is precisely why the subject found its place as the core of Jesus' high priestly prayer (John 17). Oneness reveals God's glory unlike anything else. It does this while at the same time revealing an authentic connection between believers in the body of Christ, which serves as a testimony of our connection with Christ. Jesus said, "By this all men will know that you are My disciples, if you have love for one another" (John 13:35).

An additional blessing of unity is found in this Old Testament passage penned by David:

> Behold, how good and how pleasant it is for brothers to dwell together in unity! It is like the precious oil upon the head, coming down upon the beard, even Aaron's beard, coming down upon the edge of his robes. It is like the dew of Hermon coming down upon the mountains of Zion; for there the Lord commanded the blessing—life forever (Psalm 133).

Unity is where the blessing of God rests, coming down from heaven to flow from the head to the body, and even reaching as far as the mountains of Zion. In other words, it covers everything. The reverse is also true: Where there is disunity, there is limited blessing. We cannot operate in disunity and expect the full manifestation and continuation of God's blessing in our lives. We cannot operate in disunity and expect to hear from heaven or expect God to answer our prayers in the way that both we and He long for Him to do.

Disunity—or an existence of separatism, from a spiritual perspective—is essentially at its core self-defeating and self-limiting because it reduces the movement of God's favor and blessings.

Jesus made it clear that a house divided against itself cannot stand. Whether it is your house, the church house, or the White House—division leads to destruction (Matthew 12:25). Not only that, but a spirit of dishonor can lead to this same destruction (1 Corinthians 12:22-26). Honor promotes unity while dishonor promotes division.

Put On the Belt of Truth

> Thank You, God, for the blessings You provide when I live in a spirit of oneness with others. The truth and reality of these benefits is clearly written in Your Word. As Psalm 133 states, "Behold, how good and how pleasant it is for brothers to dwell together in unity! It is like the precious oil upon the head, coming down upon the beard, even Aaron's beard, coming down upon the edge of his robes. It is like the dew of Hermon coming down upon the mountains of Zion; for there the LORD commanded the blessing—life forever." I pray that You will command the blessing upon my life and relationships. Please also help all of us in Your body to live in unity so You will command Your blessings on us as a whole. In Christ's name and by His authority, I pray this.

Put On the Breastplate of Righteousness

> Lord, I give You praise that You have not hidden righteousness from us as a mystery we must unlock. You have made it plain in our sight. Your Word tells us how we are to walk in unity, wearing the breastplate of righteousness to ward off any attacks by the enemy. Ephesians 4:1-3 states, "I, the prisoner of the Lord,

implore you to walk in a manner worthy of the calling
with which you have been called, with all humility and
gentleness, with patience, showing tolerance for one
another in love, being diligent to preserve the unity
of the Spirit in the bond of peace." Help me, and all
of us called by Your name, to preserve the unity of
the Spirit so we can enjoy and extend Your blessings.
In Christ's name and by His authority, I pray this.

Put On the Shoes of Peace

Father, I put on the shoes of unity in all I do and
say, knowing that in doing so I am promoting and
preserving peace. Peace is a blessing of unity, but
it is also a weapon of spiritual warfare. I declare
peace over my life and relationships. I declare
peace over my workplace, church, community,
and nation. Unify us in Your Spirit so we may fully
experience the peace that passes all understanding.
In Christ's name and by His authority, I pray this.

Take Up the Shield of Faith

Father God, I take up the shield of faith found in the truth
of Your Word and in the example of Jesus Christ, knowing
that if I live as He modeled for me, I will experience the
full benefits of Your blessings. Philippians 2:5-7 reminds
me of this: "Have this attitude in yourselves which was
also in Christ Jesus, who, although He existed in the
form of God, did not regard equality with God a thing
to be grasped, but emptied Himself, taking the form of
a bond-servant, and being made in the likeness of men."
Help me be of the same mind and maintain the same
love, united in spirit and intent on one purpose with all

those You have placed along my path, as Philippians 2:2 says. In Christ's name and by His authority, I pray this.

Take Up the Helmet of Salvation

Lord, comparisons breed division. When we look at other people's lives on social media and become jealous or feel lack within our own life, it only contributes to the divides built between us. The blessings of unity come when we celebrate other people's achievements and joys rather than wishing they were our own. Dig out the root of this division by helping me focus on the security that is mine in Christ Jesus. Let me be assured that my identity in Christ makes me a valued, loved, cherished child of the King. I am loved, honored, and significant in Your sight. Let each of us know this truth and find rest while wearing the helmet of salvation, which confirms our identity in Christ. In Christ's name and by His authority, I pray this.

Take Up the Sword of the Spirit

Heavenly Father, sometimes the sword of the Spirit is there to convict me of my own sins. Forgive me for how I have caused division through my own selfishness, thus limiting the amount of blessing You pour out in my life and to those around me. Your Word calls me out in 1 Corinthians 3:3, where it says, "You are still fleshly. For since there is jealousy and strife among you, are you not fleshly, and are you not walking like mere men?" I repent of jealousy and strife. I choose to embrace unity and celebrate others' accomplishments. Continue to convict my heart where I am wrong so I will be found blameless before You and You will pour out Your blessings upon my heart, mind, and life. In Christ's name and by His authority, I pray this.

16

AVOIDING TRAPS
IN AFFLUENCE

Remember what you have received and heard; and keep it, and
repent. Therefore if you do not wake up, I will come like a
thief, and you will not know at what hour I will come to you.

REVELATION 3:3

Things are certainly not always as they appear. That's why the message given to the church at Sardis in Revelation 3:1-6 is so important to understand as we look at our need for unity. This church, located just 30 miles south of Thyatira in the same general vicinity of Asia Minor, suffered from a false sense of security. They had rested their hopes on what they could see, but what they saw was not all there was to be seen.

Sardis was a city built on a high mountain where they had constructed an acropolis that made the city appear to be impregnable. It looked as if there was no way anyone could defeat this city on a hill simply because of all the trouble an army would have to go through in order to do so. Yet, the city of Sardis had been overthrown in 546 BC by Cyrus the Great after a siege followed by a surprise attack.

The reason why the attack had been successful is that the people of Sardis had become so comfortable with their own sufficiency and security that they assumed nothing could happen to them.

What was true of Sardis the city became true of Sardis the church. Which is why Jesus opened His message to the church at Sardis with this reminder of Himself: "He who has the seven Spirits of God and the seven stars, says this" (Revelation 3:1). What Jesus implied by referring to Himself in this way is that He contains the complete work of the Holy Spirit. The Christians in Sardis had become so self-sufficient in their own minds that they didn't feel they needed the Holy Spirit anymore. They thought they could do everything on their own, which is a very dangerous attitude to have.

Sound familiar? Attitudes of self-sufficiency and apathy have been growing in our churches across the land for many decades. As we become more and more affluent, we also become less and less dependent on the Holy Spirit to protect us from the enemy's advances. This blind spot has allowed divisions and judgment to creep into our churches. It has also reduced our commitment toward corporate prayer.

Do you know why Christians don't pray more? Because too many of us are too self-sufficient. We don't feel like we need God until an emergency pops up. The Christians in Sardis were educated, affluent, and at ease. As a result, they relied too heavily on themselves and became blind to the enemy's surprise attacks. One of the greatest dangers of success—whether it's related to finances, status, relationships, a career, or anything else—is that the higher you go up the ladder, the more independent you become. Why pray when you have an unlimited Mastercard? Success often lends itself to a spirit of independence that involves God only in emergencies. It also causes complacency when it comes to abiding by God's law of love and unity.

The job of the Holy Spirit is not only to energize your spiritual life, but also to make sure Satan doesn't have his way with you—especially through promoting a spirit of division in your spheres of influence. But the Holy Spirit does not do His work apart from your connection to and cooperation with Him. A life devoid of the Spirit and the unity found in Him is a life open to defeat in every area. It is just a matter of time.

Put On the Belt of Truth

> Father, Your Word tells me that the battle we fight in order to achieve an ongoing state of unity with others is a battle with the dark forces of the evil one. I know that wearing the belt of truth means recognizing who the true enemy is—an enemy who produces complacency and apathy through affluence. Ephesians 6:12 tells us, "Our struggle is not against flesh and blood, but against the rulers, against the powers, against the world forces of this darkness, against the spiritual forces of wickedness in the heavenly places." The church at Sardis had been lulled to sleep in their affluence. I pray against this outcome for the church in America and your collective body around the world. Help us all to wake up as You instructed the church at Sardis so that we might wage this war in the spiritual realm and overcome division among us. In Christ's name and by His authority, I pray this.

Put On the Breastplate of Righteousness

> God, I put on the breastplate of righteousness by taking every thought captive to Your standard of righteousness and abiding under Your rule of love. It says in 2 Corinthians 10:3-5, "Though we walk in the flesh, we do not war according to the flesh, for the weapons of our warfare are not of the flesh, but divinely powerful for the destruction of fortresses. We are destroying

speculations and every lofty thing raised up against the knowledge of God, and we are taking every thought captive to the obedience of Christ." Thank You for the weapons You provide which are divinely powerful. I know You have secured the victory if I will awaken to receive it. In Christ's name and by His authority, I pray this.

Put On the Shoes of Peace

Lord, give me discernment to understand and withstand the attacks of the enemy. The enemy attacked the people of Sardis when they assumed they were safe. Let me not grow so complacent in Your blessings that I let down my guard against the enemy's schemes. Show me how to stay mindful through a heart of peace. Let my mouth speak words of peace wherever I go. In Christ's name and by His authority, I pray this.

Take Up the Shield of Faith

With the shield of faith, Lord, we do not need to fear the enemy. Fear only contributes to the enemy's attacks. Your Word says clearly that when we are not alarmed by the enemy's attacks, this reduces his ability to attack us. We read of this in Philippians 1:27-28, where Paul encourages us to stand firm in unity: "Only conduct yourselves in a manner worthy of the gospel of Christ, so that whether I come and see you or remain absent, I will hear of you that you are standing firm in one spirit, with one mind striving together for the faith of the gospel; in no way alarmed by your opponents— which is a sign of destruction for them, but of salvation for you, and that too, from God." Our fearless unity is a sign of destruction for the enemy and all his minions. Let

faith overpower our fear and confidence replace any
concerns. In Christ's name and by His authority, I pray this.

Take Up the Helmet of Salvation

God, the helmet of salvation is my covering not only in
the day but also at night as I sleep. As we all sleep, I
pray that You will guard and watch over us so that
the enemy does not have the opportunity to disrupt
or overpower us. Guard us securely in the salvation
which has been provided to us by the blood of Jesus
Christ. In Christ's name and by His authority, I pray this.

Take Up the Sword of the Spirit

Father, the Word of God calls us as the body of Christ
to remain sober in spirit. It is easy to let our guard down
against the enemy's attacks when we are affluent and at
ease. But 1 Peter 5:8 is the sword which reminds us, "Be
of sober spirit, be on the alert. Your adversary, the devil,
prowls around like a roaring lion, seeking someone to
devour." May we not be devoured in the midst of the
blessings You have given us. May we escape the trap of
the evil one as a bird escapes a trap set for him. Psalm
124:7 is the sword I lift against the lies of Satan: "Our
soul has escaped as a bird out of the snare of the trapper;
the snare is broken and we have escaped." Yes, the
snares of affluence, fear, and division are broken and
we, bought with the blood of Jesus Christ, have escaped.
In Christ's name and by His authority, I pray this.

17

PURPOSEFUL PRAYER

*If calamity comes upon us, whether the sword of judgment,
or plague or famine, we will stand in your presence before
this temple that bears your Name and will cry out to you
in our distress, and you will hear us and save us.*

2 Chronicles 20:9 (niv)

f you have ever felt powerless in this area of overcoming divisions
and preserving unity, you are in good company. In fact, you are
keeping company with Judah's king. Listen to Jehoshaphat's words of
powerlessness: "Our God, will You not judge them? For we are powerless before this vast number that comes to fight against us. We do
not know what to do" (2 Chronicles 20:12 hcsb).

Jehoshaphat had become weak in his knees, and his only hope
at this point was a miracle. What a perfect example for us to look at
when we are facing such a seemingly insurmountable challenge as
bridging the divides between us. We can note what the king did and
apply it in our own personal lives as we seek unity. Jehoshaphat's
problem turned him toward purposeful prayer. He used his lips to
gain the victory he sought. Now, that's an interesting battle strategy
for a king.

Yahweh, the God of our ancestors, are You not the God who is in heaven, and do You not rule over all the kingdoms of the nations? Power and might are in Your hand, and no one can stand against You. Are You not our God who drove out the inhabitants of this land before Your people Israel and who gave it forever to the descendants of Abraham Your friend? They have lived in the land and have built You a sanctuary in it for Your name and have said, "If disaster comes on us—sword or judgment, pestilence or famine—we will stand before this temple and before You, for Your name is in this temple. We will cry out to You because of our distress, and You will hear and deliver" (2 Chronicles 20:6-9 HCSB).

Prayer is an invitation to heaven to address something going wrong on earth. It's calling on eternity to visit time. It's giving heavenly permission for earthly intervention. Prayer is not the pregame; it is the game. It is not the preparation for battle; it is the war. Every significant movement in the history of Christianity was birthed first and foremost in prayer. That's the approach this king took when his nation was surrounded by enemies. Jehoshaphat strategically cried out to God. Let's look at the anatomy of the king's prayer.

The king begins by reminding God who He is.

Then he reminds God about what He has said.

After this, he introduces God to the problem he is facing.

The order of this prayer is important because it puts things in the proper perspective. Jehoshaphat begins by acknowledging the greatness of God—declaring His power and ability—before diving into his difficulties. When we face the big problem of division, we need something that can give us an even bigger solution—and that something is God. We will never discover that God is all we need until God is all we have.

When a problem is so big that there is no earthly solution to fix it, you can see God work in ways that will blow your mind. This is what happened to King Jehoshaphat, and it began when the king addressed God first and foremost as great. If your view of God is small, then He will be your last resort in a difficult situation. After all, you don't really expect too much from Him. But if your view of God is great—as was the king's—you will turn to Him to deliver you, and you will begin by reminding Him of His greatness.

Jehoshaphat's response to his situation reveals another thing we can do when we're overwhelmed by disunity—we can hold God hostage to His Word. Most believers do not realize this, but you can actually hold God hostage to what He has said. You can throw His words right back at Him because He is faithful to what He has said. This is exactly what King Jehoshaphat did in his prayer. He reminded God of what He said would happen when enemies came upon them. If they would go to His house and cry out to Him, He would hear and deliver them. Essentially, Jehoshaphat said, "Remember what You said, God? Because I'm doing that right now." May we do the same when we pray for unity.

Put On the Belt of Truth

Lord, prayer is a powerful tool we can use as the body of Christ in order to overcome division and usher in a period of unity. I believe in prayer, but I also want to ask that You open more people's hearts to the power of prayer as well. I hold fast to the truth found in 1 John 5:15, which says, "If we know that He hears us in whatever we ask, we know that we have the requests which we have asked from Him." When we ask You to bridge the divides and heal the wounds that separate us, we know You hear us. We know You are granting

our request for unity. Bring healing to our hearts, Lord.
Bring unity into our churches and among us as people.
In Christ's name and by His authority, I pray this.

Put On the Breastplate of Righteousness

Father, Paul prayed for the believers, asking that the
eyes of their hearts would be enlightened. We read
in Ephesians 1:18, "I pray that the eyes of your heart
may be enlightened, so that you will know what is the
hope of His calling, what are the riches of the glory
of His inheritance in the saints." I pray now in the
same sentiment for all believers on the planet today.
Enlighten the eyes of our hearts so we can understand
true righteousness in unity. We cannot take up the
breastplate of righteousness if we are blinded to the
effects of division among us. Remove the blinders and
awaken our souls to Your healing and unifying power.
In Christ's name and by His authority, I pray this.

Put On the Shoes of Peace

I come to You in praise for what I know You can and will
do through the prayers of Your people. Usher in a time
of peace in our hearts. Block the divisions before they
even have time to spring up. Cast out the enemy from
our midst. Cleanse Your body of believers by stripping
us of the selfishness that leads to accusation, blame,
jealousy, and everything else that divides us. None
of us can throw the first stone because all of us are
saved by the same blood of Christ. Jesus, You are our
peace, as Ephesians 2:14 says. Help us win this battle
and overcome division as we walk in Your footsteps of
peace. In Christ's name and by His authority, I pray this.

Take Up the Shield of Faith

Father, I take up the shield of faith, believing that what
You said in Jeremiah 29:12 remains true in our situation
as we seek to overcome divisions throughout the world
today: "You will call upon Me and come and pray to Me,
and I will listen to you." Thank You for listening to us as
we call on You. We ask for Your intervention to defeat the
enemy who stokes division like flames for fighting. Make
Your name great in our hearts as we look to You in faith.
You also said in Jeremiah 33:3, "Call to Me and I will
answer you, and I will tell you great and mighty things,
which you do not know." Tell us the great and mighty
things which will open the doors for unity and oneness to
thrive. In Christ's name and by His authority, I pray this.

Take Up the Helmet of Salvation

Lord, Your helmet of salvation protects me from giving
up. It's so easy to hear the news or watch talk shows or
listen to podcasts and feel as if there is no solution to that
which divides us as people. It is impossible to miss the
divisions in my workplace and even my own home. But
Lord, I take courage in knowing that the same sacrifice
which was sufficient to purchase my salvation is enough
to win this battle against the enemy. Remind me of the
power of the helmet of salvation when I become weary
and want to throw in the towel. Remind me that victory
is secured by You, in Your name and for Your great
glory. In Christ's name and by His authority, I pray this.

Take Up the Sword of the Spirit

Lord, Jesus prayed for those who follow Him and the
divisions we face in our relationships, communities,

nation, and world. He prayed in John 17:15, "I do not ask You to take them out of the world, but to keep them from the evil one." Keep us from the evil one, Lord. Let Jesus' prayer surround us with Your protection and victory. Show us how to remain in the world but not succumb to the devastation of the world. Give us wisdom on how to overcome division. For it is written in James 1:5, "If any of you lacks wisdom, let him ask of God, who gives to all generously and without reproach, and it will be given to him." It is also written in 1 John 4:4, "You are from God, little children, and have overcome them; because greater is He who is in you than he who is in the world." I stand firmly on Your Word. May it be done just as You have said. In Christ's name and by His authority, I pray this.

18

SEASONED WITH GRACE

*Let your conversation be always full of grace, seasoned with
salt, so that you may know how to answer everyone.*

Colossians 4:6 (niv)

Dynamite is powerful. It can be used to blow things apart. We all
have a similar power within ourselves. We have access to something so strong—for good or for evil—that we bring life or death into
situations on a regular basis. What's worrisome about this, though, is
that most of us do not realize this power. And far too many of us let
it ride roughshod over other people in our lives.

You and I were created by God with access to an internal, explo-
sive power that can construct or destroy. It is the dynamite in our
dentures—the tool known as the tongue. The mouth has the power
to destroy anything and everything in its path. The muscle in your
mouth is no small thing. In fact, relationships have ended because
of the sticks of dynamite that continue to blow up their connection.
There are loved ones who have not spoken to each other for years
because the blast was so big and the pain was so deep, they have been
unable to recover. Social media allows the spark of this dynamite to

spread like a wildfire, destroying everything in its path. As believers in Christ, we can do better.

God might not use soap on our tongues to steer us in the right direction concerning this critical source of life or death in our mouths, but He does ask us to use some salt. "Your speech should always be gracious, seasoned with salt, so that you may know how you should answer each person," writes Paul in his letter to the church at Colossae (Colossians 4:6 HCSB). Or if you don't prefer salt, He suggests some honey: "Pleasant words are a honeycomb: sweet to the taste and health to the body" (Proverbs 16:24 HCSB).

In the book of Deuteronomy, Moses says, "I call heaven and earth as witnesses against you today that I have set before you life and death, blessing and curse. Choose life so that you and your descendants may live" (30:19 HCSB). When he speaks of "life and death," he is not referring to killing people physically. He means they can choose to bring blessing or destruction through their choices, and that would include their choice of words.

You, too, can bring unity or division. You can bring oneness or separation. Your words matter greatly.

A surgeon uses a scalpel to help preserve life, but a criminal can use the same sharpened blade to bring death. A wise doctor can use a syringe to promote healing in a sick patient, but a drug pusher can use the same syringe to cause death. You and I also have the power to bring life or death, blessing or a curse, unity or division into the lives around us simply through our mouths.

Whenever you speak a word that disagrees with God's Word—even though you use God's name—Satan has poisoned your speech. Man's natural interests agree with Satan's interests. Any interest apart from God as Lord, Master, and Ruler is Satan's interest. When you come to realize how often your everyday conversations disagree with God's Word and His truth—through complaining, backbiting, judging, divisive speech, or the like—you will understand why your speech may be blocking your ability to promote unity.

Your words are simply vocalizations of your thoughts and beliefs. When you come to understand that your words have the power to invite either God or Satan into a conversation, you will want to season your words with grace, unity, and life. Satan loves to create a conflict of interest between your will and God's will. Satan's strategy is always division. But once you realize your words have the power to overcome his strategy, you will use them to bring about unity where division once dominated.

Put On the Belt of Truth

> Lord, thank You for the power You have placed within our words. You have given me the ability to speak words that affirm love, unity, and oneness and spread grace. In fact, Your Word reminds me to do just that in Ephesians 4:29, which says, "Let no unwholesome word proceed from your mouth, but only such a word as is good for edification according to the need of the moment, so that it will give grace to those who hear." Help me "give grace" to everyone I come across. Help me "give grace" through everything I post, share, or comment on through my social media accounts. Let my life be an instrument of grace and truth so I can be used by You to encourage unity among all. In Christ's name and by His authority, I pray this.

Put On the Breastplate of Righteousness

> Father, righteousness is to spring from my mouth. Pure words of love, unity, and hope are to be the norm of my speech. Jesus described the importance of speaking rightly when He said in Matthew 15:11, "It is not what enters into the mouth that defiles the

man, but what proceeds out of the mouth, this defiles the man." You have given me the power to speak righteousness into my surroundings. Help me use that power to bring good and oneness to all. In Christ's name and by His authority, I pray this.

Put On the Shoes of Peace

Heavenly Father, I pray for peace in my mouth and the words I speak. Let my words create a pathway of peace not only for myself, but for everyone with whom I come into contact. Show me how I can intentionally speak of peace, grace, and unity more frequently. Give me wisdom and insight on how to be a vessel of peace and unity through my speech. Let me honor You with all I have, and let that start with my heart and words. In Christ's name and by His authority, I pray this.

Take Up the Shield of Faith

Lord, you have reminded us in Proverbs 21:23 that "he who guards his mouth and his tongue, guards his soul from troubles." I take up the shield of faith as I place my trust in Your Word, knowing that when I guard my mouth and tongue, I am also guarding my soul from trouble. I know that Your Word will protect me, and when I follow it, I will benefit from it. As Proverbs 18:20-21 states, "With the fruit of a man's mouth his stomach will be satisfied; he will be satisfied with the product of his lips. Death and life are in the power of the tongue, and those who love it will eat its fruit." I desire to eat the fruit of life through what I speak, according to the pursuit of unity and love in the body of Christ. In Christ's name and by His authority, I pray this.

Take Up the Helmet of Salvation

Father, You have saved us for Yourself with the goal of increasing the love we have for You and the love we have for each other. Love is displayed in unity and trust. Help me trust in Your salvation so I do not speak words of doubt, confusion, or loss. Help me speak confidently concerning Your will for all of us to be unified. Help me frame my words with certainty, knowing You will enable us to do what You have called us to do. Help us all turn our words away from complaints, blame, hate speech, and divisiveness and instead speak words of life, grace, and unity. In Christ's name and by His authority, I pray this.

Take Up the Sword of the Spirit

It is written in Luke 6:45, "The good man out of the good treasure of his heart brings forth what is good; and the evil man out of the evil treasure brings forth what is evil; for his mouth speaks from that which fills his heart." I choose to produce good treasures in this area of unity in my personal life, my workplace, my church, my community, and this nation. It is written in Proverbs 31:26, "She opens her mouth in wisdom, and the teaching of kindness is on her tongue." May we all open our mouths in wisdom and allow the teaching of kindness to be on our tongues at all times, in all ways, toward all people. This will usher in an age of unity like we have never experienced before. In Christ's name and by His authority, I pray this.

THE POWER OF FASTING

We often forget to eat because we are busy or distracted, but the Lord asks us to forgo eating intentionally when He calls us to fast. Fasting is a deliberate abstinence from some form of physical gratification, for a period of time, in order to achieve a greater spiritual goal. The second half of this definition is crucial, because fasting without prayer is just a diet. Fasting is your way of telling God that your need for His intervention is so great, and you are so passionate about it, that you are willing to sacrifice your physical needs for the answer.

Jesus made a powerful statement about the importance of the spiritual over the physical when He told His disciples, "I have food to eat that you do not know about" (John 4:32). He was dealing with the spiritual needs of the woman at the well and her entire village, which were far more important to Him than eating the food the disciples had brought Him. Fasting shows God that our need for Him is greater than our need for food (or whatever item we choose to abstain from). In Matthew 4:1-11, Jesus went into the wilderness to be tested by the devil. After Jesus prepared by fasting for 40 days, the devil came to Him and tempted Him to eat, but Jesus quoted Deuteronomy 8:3: "Man does not live by bread alone, but man lives by everything that proceeds out of the mouth of the LORD."

We can't live on food alone because we need the Word of God even more. Fasting shows God and ourselves that His Word is more important than food. When we fast, we give the Holy Spirit our full attention. The experience leads to a brokenness that shouts, "I can't do this!" The self-sufficient man or woman won't fast, but the desperate one will. The self-sufficient church won't fast, but the desperate one will. The self-sufficient nation won't fast, but the desperate one will.

We have reached such enormous levels of division in our personal lives, churches, communities, nation, and the world that we must fast and pray for a wave of unity to wash over us all.

The truth is we cannot usher in oneness in our own strength. We can't force unity simply by strategizing. We've got to starve our flesh to feed our spirit. When our spirits are strong and our flesh is weak, huge spiritual breakthroughs occur. Isaiah 58:6-9 promises that when we fast the way God intended, our light will shine, healing will come quickly to our land, and the Lord will answer when we call.

The question is not whether fasting makes a difference. The question is, *How badly do you want a difference to be made?*

Fasting usually involves setting aside food, although we can fast from any physical appetite, including sex within marriage (1 Corinthians 7:5). We can fast from the hours we spend watching television or surfing the Internet. The idea is to devote the time we would ordinarily spend on these activities to prayer and waiting before the Lord.

Fasting calls us to renounce the natural in order to invoke the supernatural. When you fast, you say no to yourself so you can hear a yes from God in a time of need or crisis—like the one our nation is facing. A collective fast throughout the body of Christ on behalf of our land sends a message to our Lord that we are wanting and waiting to hear from Him.

Fasting is a major principle throughout the Bible. People in Scripture often fasted in situations that demanded a spiritual breakthrough. In Zechariah 7:5-6, the Lord said, "When you fasted and mourned in the fifth and seventh months these seventy years, was it actually for Me that you fasted? When you eat and drink, do you not eat for yourselves and do you not drink for yourselves?"

Even though the fasts God referred to here would have been unnecessary if His people had repented, these verses still give us an important principle about fasting. When we eat, we eat for ourselves, with nothing more than our own satisfaction in mind. But when we fast, we should do so with God in mind, for His pleasure. When we fast, God says, "This is for Me."

So often we feed the body while starving the soul. But when we fast, we give the soul a higher priority than the body. We are asking God to interact with our souls. Are you willing to give up feeding your flesh for a time in order to gain unity in your relationships, your church, and our land?

The Purpose of Fasting

According to Isaiah 58:4, the purpose of fasting is "to make your voice heard on high." When we fast with the proper motivation, our voice is heard in heaven. That is, we come into God's presence in a powerful way. Imagine what would happen if your church came together as a body to collectively fast and call on God to end the divisions present in your church and community.

The nature of fasting demands concentrated effort and time to come into God's presence. Think about the effort we make to eat when we're hungry. Most of us will make a way where there is no way when it's mealtime because we are desperate to satisfy our hunger. When we fast, we are desperate to satisfy something much deeper—a spiritual need.

When we fast, God sharpens our spiritual focus so we can see things more clearly. In 1 Thessalonians 5:23, Paul prayed that his readers would be sanctified and preserved in their "spirit and soul and body." Paul's order here is purposeful. We are not made up of body, soul, and spirit, but spirit, soul, and body. We are created to live from the inside out, not from the outside in.

You ask, "Why is that important?" Because if you look at yourself as a body that happens to house a soul and spirit, you will live for your body first. But if you understand that you are spirit at the core of your being, you will live for the spirit. If we want to really live, the spirit—the inner person—must be set free. Our spirits must be cracked open to release the Spirit's life, and fasting helps us do this.

Far too often, our problem is that we aren't ready for God to work in our spirit. We make all kinds of resolutions and promises, which are really just ways of saying to God, "I can do this myself." But if we could do it, we would have already done it.

One of the primary reasons our relationships, churches, and culture are so divided today is that we have become self-sufficient. We refuse to humble ourselves collectively before the Lord in order to fast and pray and seek His movement in our spirits. What God wants to hear us say is, "Lord, we can't do this. We've tried everything we know and we can't fix our lives. Lord, we throw our inability and our failure at Your feet."

God says, "Now I can do something."

When we fail to humble ourselves before God, we wind up trying to live the Christian life in our own power. We call on our flesh to help us defeat the flesh—which is a contradiction in terms. Fasting is a tangible way of demonstrating to God that we are setting aside the flesh in order to deal with the spirit.

More than that, fasting is also a way of prostrating ourselves before God. In the Bible, when people were broken before the Lord, they often fell on their faces. They put ashes on their heads and tore their clothes as a way of saying, "Lord, I can't do anything. I am at the end of my rope."

God wants us to reach that point so He can demonstrate His power and get all the glory, which He deserves. The apostle James says those who humble themselves before God will be lifted up (James 4:10). Fasting puts us on the path of humility.

The bottom line is that when we fast, we will get God's undivided attention: "You will call, and the LORD will answer; you will cry, and He will say, 'Here I am'" (Isaiah 58:9). You may say, "But I've been calling to God all this time." Are you calling to Him with a fast? Remember, fasting makes your voice heard on high. God wants to be treated seriously.

SCRIPTURES ON OUR UNITY IN CHRIST

Genesis

A man shall leave his father and his mother, and be joined to his wife; and they shall become one flesh (2:24).

Deuteronomy

Hear, O Israel! The LORD is our God, the LORD is one! (6:4).

2 Chronicles

The hand of God was also on Judah to give them one heart to do what the king and the princes commanded by the word of the LORD (30:12).

Psalms

Behold, how good and how pleasant it is for brothers to dwell together in unity! (133:1).

Ecclesiastes

Two are better than one because they have a good return for their labor. For if either of them falls, the one will lift up his companion. But woe to the one who falls when there is not another to lift him up. Furthermore, if two lie down together they keep warm, but how can one be warm alone? And if one can overpower him who is alone, two can resist him. A cord of three strands is not quickly torn apart (4:9-12).

Amos

Do two men walk together unless they have made an appointment? (3:3).

Matthew

Knowing their thoughts Jesus said to them, "Any kingdom divided against itself is laid waste; and any city or house divided against itself will not stand" (12:25).

If your brother sins, go and show him his fault in private; if he listens to you, you have won your brother (18:15).

If two of you agree on earth about anything that they may ask, it shall be done for them by My Father who is in heaven. For where two or three have gathered together in My name, I am there in their midst (18:19-20).

Do not be called Rabbi; for One is your Teacher, and you are all brothers (23:8).

John

I am no longer in the world; and yet they themselves are in the world, and I come to You. Holy Father, keep them in Your name, the name which You have given Me, that they may be one even as We are (17:11).

I do not ask on behalf of these alone, but for those also who believe in Me through their word; that they may all be one; even as You, Father, are in Me and I in You, that they also may be in Us, so that the world may believe that You sent Me. The glory which You have given Me I have given to them, that they may be one, just as We are one; I in them and You in Me, that they may be perfected in unity, so that the world may know that You sent Me, and loved them, even as You have loved Me (17:20-23).

Acts

The congregation of those who believed were of one heart and soul; and not one of them claimed that anything belonging to him was his own, but all things were common property to them (4:32).

Be on guard for yourselves and for all the flock, among which the Holy Spirit has made you overseers, to shepherd the church of God which He purchased with His own blood (20:28).

Romans

Just as we have many members in one body and all the members do not have the same function, so we, who are many, are one body in Christ, and individually members one of another (12:4-5).

Be devoted to one another in brotherly love; give preference to one another in honor (12:10).

Be of the same mind toward one another; do not be haughty in mind, but associate with the lowly. Do not be wise in your own estimation (12:16).

If possible, so far as it depends on you, be at peace with all men (12:18).

To this end Christ died and lived again, that He might be Lord both of the dead and of the living (14:9).

Now may the God who gives perseverance and encouragement grant you to be of the same mind with one another according to Christ Jesus, so that with one accord you may with one voice glorify the God and Father of our Lord Jesus Christ. Therefore, accept one another, just as Christ also accepted us to the glory of God (15:5-7).

1 Corinthians

Now I exhort you, brethren, by the name of our Lord Jesus Christ, that you all agree and that there be no divisions among you, but that you be made complete in the same mind and in the same judgment (1:10).

Even as the body is one and yet has many members, and all the members of the body, though they are many, are one body, so also is Christ. For by one Spirit we were all baptized into one body, whether Jews or Greeks, whether slaves or free, and we were all made to drink of one Spirit (12:12-13).

If one member suffers, all the members suffer with it; if one member is honored, all the members rejoice with it (12:26).

2 Corinthians

Finally, brethren, rejoice, be made complete, be comforted, be like-minded, live in peace; and the God of love and peace will be with you (13:11).

Galatians

There is neither Jew nor Greek, there is neither slave nor free man, there is neither male nor female; for you are all one in Christ Jesus (3:28).

Ephesians

He made known to us the mystery of His will, according to His kind intention which He purposed in Him with a view to an administration suitable to the fullness of the times, that is, the summing up of all things in Christ, things in the heavens and things on the earth (1:9-10).

He Himself is our peace, who made both groups into one and broke down the barrier of the dividing wall (2:14).

Being diligent to preserve the unity of the Spirit in the bond of peace. There is one body and one Spirit, just as also you were called in one hope of your calling; one Lord, one faith, one baptism, one God and Father of all who is over all and through all and in all (4:3-6).

Until we all attain to the unity of the faith, and of the knowledge of the Son of God, to a mature man, to the measure of the stature which belongs to the fullness of Christ (4:13).

We are to grow up in all aspects into Him who is the head, even Christ, from whom the whole body, being fitted and held together by what every joint supplies, according to the proper working of each individual part, causes the growth of the body for the building up of itself in love (4:15-16).

Be kind to one another, tender-hearted, forgiving each other, just as God in Christ also has forgiven you (4:32).

Philippians

Only conduct yourselves in a manner worthy of the gospel of Christ, so that whether I come and see you or remain absent, I will hear of you that you are standing firm in one spirit, with one mind striving together for the faith of the gospel (1:27).

If there is any encouragement in Christ, if there is any consolation of love, if there is any fellowship of the Spirit, if any affection and compassion, make my joy complete by being of the same mind, maintaining the same love, united in spirit, intent on one purpose. Do nothing from selfishness or empty conceit, but with humility of mind regard one another as more important than yourselves; do not merely look out for your own personal interests, but also for the interests of others (2:1-4).

Colossians

Beyond all these things put on love, which is the perfect bond of unity. Let the peace of Christ rule in your hearts, to which indeed you were called in one body; and be thankful. Let the word of Christ richly dwell within you, with all wisdom teaching and admonishing one another with psalms and hymns and spiritual songs, singing with thankfulness in your hearts to God. Whatever you do in word or deed, do all in the name of the Lord Jesus, giving thanks through Him to God the Father (3:14-17).

Titus

Reject a factious man after a first and second warning, knowing that such a man is perverted and is sinning, being self-condemned (3:10-11).

Hebrews

Let us consider how to stimulate one another to love and good deeds, not forsaking our own assembling together, as is the habit of some, but encouraging one another; and all the more as you see the day drawing near (10:24-25).

James

Where jealousy and selfish ambition exist, there is disorder and every evil thing (3:16).

1 Peter

To sum up, all of you be harmonious, sympathetic, brotherly, kindhearted, and humble in spirit (3:8).

1 John

Beloved, if God so loved us, we also ought to love one another. No one has seen God at any time; if we love one another, God abides in us, and His love is perfected in us (4:11-12).

APPENDIX:
THE URBAN ALTERNATIVE

The Urban Alternative (TUA) equips, empowers, and unites Christians to impact individuals, families, churches, and communities through a thoroughly kingdom agenda worldview. In teaching truth, we seek to transform lives.

The core cause of the problems we face in our personal lives, homes, churches, and societies is a spiritual one; therefore, the only way to address it is spiritually. We've tried a political, social, economic, and even a religious agenda.

It's time for a **Kingdom agenda**.

The Kingdom agenda can be defined as the visible manifestation of the comprehensive rule of God over every area of life.

The unifying central theme throughout the Bible is the glory of God and the advancement of His kingdom. The conjoining thread from Genesis to Revelation—from beginning to end—is focused on one thing: God's glory through advancing God's kingdom.

When you do not have that theme, the Bible becomes disconnected stories that are great for inspiration but seem to be unrelated in purpose and direction. The Bible exists to share God's movement in history toward the establishment and expansion of His kingdom, highlighting the connectivity throughout, which is the kingdom. Understanding that increases the relevancy of this several-thousand-year-old manuscript to your day-to-day living, because the kingdom is not only then, it is now.

The absence of the kingdom's influence in our personal and family lives, churches, and communities has led to a deterioration in our world of immense proportions:

- People live segmented, compartmentalized lives because they lack God's kingdom worldview.

- Families disintegrate because they exist for their own satisfaction rather than for the kingdom.

- Churches are limited in the scope of their impact because they fail to comprehend that the goal of the church is not the church itself, but the kingdom.

- Communities have nowhere to turn to find real solutions for real people who have real problems because the church has become divided, ingrown, and unable to transform the cultural landscape in any relevant way.

The kingdom agenda offers us a way to see and live life with a solid hope by optimizing the solutions of heaven. When God, and His rule, is no longer the final and authoritative standard under which all else falls, order and hope leaves with Him. But the reverse of that is true as well: As long as you have God, you have hope. If God is still in the picture, and as long as His agenda is still on the table, it's not over.

Even if relationships collapse, God will sustain you. Even if finances dwindle, God will keep you. Even if dreams die, God will revive you. As long as God, and His rule, is still the overarching rule in your life, family, church, and community, there is always hope.

Our world needs the King's agenda. Our churches need the King's agenda. Our families need the King's agenda.

In many major cities, there is a loop that drivers can take when they want to get somewhere on the other side of the city but don't necessarily want to head straight through downtown. This loop will take you close enough to the city so that you can see its towering buildings and skyline, but not close enough to actually experience it.

This is precisely what we, as a culture, have done with God. We have put Him on the "loop" of our personal, family, church, and community lives. He's close enough to be at hand should we need Him in an emergency, but far enough away that He can't be the center of who we are.

We want God on the "loop," not the King of the Bible who comes downtown into the very heart of our ways. Leaving God on the "loop" brings about dire consequences as we have seen in our own lives and with others. But when we make God, and His rule, the centerpiece of all we think, do, or say, it is then that we will experience Him in the way He longs to be experienced by us.

He wants us to be kingdom people with kingdom minds set on fulfilling His kingdom's purposes. He wants us to pray, as Jesus did, "Not my will, but Thy will be done." Because His is the kingdom, the power, and the glory.

There is only one God, and we are not Him. As King and Creator, God calls the shots. It is only when we align ourselves underneath His comprehensive hand that we will access His full power and authority in all spheres of life: personal, familial, church, and community.

As we learn how to govern ourselves under God, we then transform the institutions of family, church, and society from a biblically based kingdom worldview.

Under Him, we touch heaven and change earth.

To achieve our goal, we use a variety of strategies, approaches, and resources for reaching and equipping as many people as possible.

Broadcast Media

Millions of individuals experience *The Alternative with Dr. Tony Evans* through the daily radio broadcast playing on nearly **1,400 RADIO outlets** and in over **130 countries**. The broadcast can also be seen on several television networks, and is viewable online at TonyEvans.org. You can also listen or view the daily broadcast by downloading the Tony Evans app for free in the App store. Over 20,000,000 message downloads/streams occur each year.

Leadership Training

The Tony Evans Training Center (TETC) facilitates educational programming that embodies the ministry philosophy of Dr. Tony Evans as expressed through the kingdom agenda. The training courses focus on leadership development and discipleship in the following five tracks:

- Bible and Theology
- Personal Growth
- Family and Relationships
- Church Health and Leadership Development
- Society and Community Impact Strategies

The TETC program includes courses for both local and online students. Furthermore, TETC programming includes coursework for nonstudent attendees. Pastors, Christian leaders and Christian laity, both local and at a distance, can seek out The Kingdom Agenda Certificate for personal, spiritual and professional development. For more information, visit: tonyevanstraining.org

The Kingdom Agenda Pastors (KAP) provides a *viable network* for *like-minded pastors* who embrace the Kingdom Agenda philosophy. Pastors have the opportunity to go deeper with Dr. Tony Evans as they are given greater biblical knowledge, practical applications, and resources to impact individuals, families, churches, and communities. KAP welcomes *senior and associate pastors* of all churches. KAP also offers an annual Summit held each year in Dallas with intensive seminars, workshops, and resources.

Pastors' Wives Ministry, founded by Dr. Lois Evans, provides *counsel, encouragement*, and *spiritual resources* for pastors' wives as they serve with their husbands in the ministry. A primary focus of the ministry is the KAP Summit that offers senior pastors' wives a safe place to *reflect, renew*, and *relax* along with training in personal development, spiritual growth, and care for their emotional and physical well-being.

Community and Cultural Influence

National Church Adopt-A-School Initiative (NCAASI) prepares churches across the country to impact communities by using *public schools as the primary vehicle for effecting positive social change* in urban youth and families. Leaders of churches, school districts, faith-based organizations, and other nonprofit organizations are equipped with the knowledge and tools to *forge partnerships* and build *strong social service delivery systems*. This training is based on the comprehensive church-based community impact strategy conducted by Oak Cliff Bible Fellowship. It addresses such areas as economic development, education, housing, health revitalization, family renewal, and racial reconciliation. We assist churches in tailoring the model to meet specific needs of their communities while simultaneously addressing the spiritual and moral frame of reference. Training events are held annually in the Dallas area at Oak Cliff Bible Fellowship.

Athlete's Impact (AI) exists as an outreach both into and through the sports arena. Coaches are the most influential factor in young people's lives, even ahead of their parents. With the growing rise of fatherlessness in our culture, more young people are looking to their coaches for guidance, character development, practical needs, and hope. After coaches on the influencer scale fall athletes. Athletes (whether professional or amateur) influence younger athletes and kids within their spheres of impact. Knowing this, we have made it our aim to equip and train coaches and athletes on how to live out and utilize their God-given roles for the benefit of the kingdom. We aim to do this through our iCoach App as well as resources such as The Playbook: A Life Strategy Guide for Athletes.

Tony Evans Films ushers in positive life change through compelling video-shorts, animation, and feature-length films. We seek to build kingdom disciples through the power of story. We use a variety of platforms for viewer consumption and have over 35,000,000 digital views. We also merge video-shorts and film with relevant Bible study materials to bring people to the saving knowledge of Jesus Christ and to strengthen the body of Christ worldwide. Tony Evans Films released the first feature-length film, *Kingdom Men Rising*, in April, 2019, in over 800 theaters nationwide, in partnership with Lifeway Films. The second release, *Journey with Jesus*, in partnership with Right Now Media and filmed in Israel, made its nationwide theatrical debut in Fall 2020.

Resource Development

We are fostering lifelong learning partnerships with the people we serve by providing a variety of published materials. Dr. Evans has published more than 100 unique titles based on over 50 years of preaching whether that is in booklet, book, or Bible study format. He also holds the honor of writing and publishing the first full-Bible commentary and study Bible by an African-American, released in 2019. This Bible sits in permanent display as an historic release in the Museum of the Bible in Washington, D.C.

For more information, and a complimentary copy of
Dr. Evans' devotional newsletter,
call (800) 800-3222
or write TUA at P.O. Box 4000, Dallas TX 75208,
or visit us online
www.TonyEvans.org

NOTES

1. *Lexico*, s.v. "empathy," accessed September 27, 2019, http://www.lexico.com/en/definition/empathy.

2. *Lexico*, s.v. "sympathy," accessed September 27, 2019, http://www.lexico.com/en/definition/sympathy.

Building kingdom disciples.

At **The Urban Alternative,** our heart is to build kingdom disciples—a vision that starts with the individual and expands to the family, the church and the nation. The nearly 50-year teaching ministry of Tony Evans has allowed us to reach a world in need with:

The Alternative – Our flagship radio program brings hope and comfort to an audience of millions on over 1,400 radio outlets across the country.

tonyevans.org – Our library of teaching resources provides solid Bible teaching through the inspirational books and sermons of Tony Evans.

Tony Evans Training Center – Experience the adventure of God's Word with our online classroom, providing at-your-own-pace courses for your PC or mobile device. Visit tonyevanstraining.org.

Tony Evans app – This popular resource for finding inspiration on-the-go has had over 20,000,000 launches. It's packed with audio and video clips, devotionals, Scripture readings and dozens of other tools.

tonyevans.org

Life is busy,
but Bible study is still possible.

*a **portable** seminary*

Explore the kingdom.
Anytime, anywhere.

tonyevanstraining.o

*Subscription model

MORE GREAT
HARVEST HOUSE BOOKS BY
DR. TONY EVANS

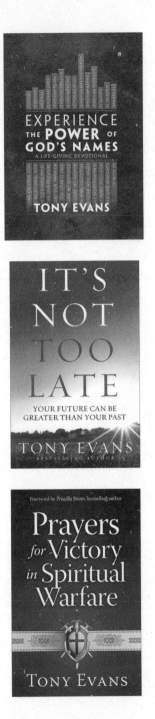

EXPERIENCE
THE POWER OF
GOD'S NAMES
A LIFE-GIVING DEVOTIONAL

TONY EVANS

EXPERIENCING
GOD
TOGETHER
How Your Connection with Others Deepens
Your Relationship with God

TONY EVANS

IT'S
NOT
TOO
LATE
YOUR FUTURE CAN BE
GREATER THAN YOUR PAST

TONY EVANS
BESTSELLING AUTHOR

THE POWER OF
GOD'S NAMES

TONY EVANS
BESTSELLING AUTHOR

Foreword by Priscilla Shirer, bestselling author

Prayers
for Victory
in Spiritual
Warfare

TONY EVANS

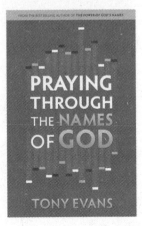

FROM THE BESTSELLING AUTHOR OF THE POWER OF GOD'S NAMES

PRAYING
THROUGH
THE NAMES
OF GOD

TONY EVANS

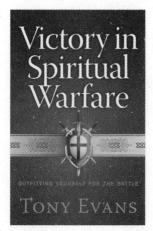

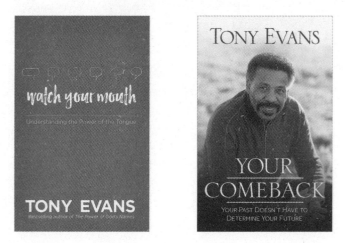